PETER

Peter Ackroyd is an award-winning historian, biographer, novelist, poet and broadcaster. He is the author of the acclaimed non-fiction bestsellers *London: The Biography, Thames: Sacred River* and *London Under*; biographies of figures including Charles Dickens, William Blake, Charlie Chaplin and Alfred Hitchcock; and a multi-volume history of England. He has won the Whitbread Biography Award, the Royal Society of Literature's William Heinemann Award, the James Tait Black Memorial Prize, the Guardian Fiction Prize, the Somerset Maugham Award and the South Bank Prize for Literature. He holds a CBE for services to literature.

ALSO BY PETER ACKROYD

Non-Fiction

London: The Biography
Albion: The Origins of the English Imagination
The Collection: Journalism, Reviews, Essays, Short Stories, Lectures, edited by Thomas Wright
Thames: Sacred River
Venice: Pure City
The English Ghost

Fiction

The Great Fire of London
The Last Testament of Oscar Wilde
Hawksmoor
Chatterton
First Light
English Music
The House of Doctor Dee
Dan Leno and the Limehouse Golem
Milton in America
The Plato Papers
The Clerkenwell Tales
The Lambs of London
The Fall of Troy
The Casebook of Victor Frankenstein
Three Brothers

Biography

Ezra Pound and his World
T. S. Eliot
Dickens
Blake
The Life of Thomas More
Shakespeare: The Biography

Brief Lives

Chaucer
J. M. W. Turner
Newton
Poe: A Life Cut Short
Wilkie Collins
Charlie Chaplin
Alfred Hitchcock

PETER ACKROYD

Queer City

Gay London from the Romans to the present day

VINTAGE

1 3 5 7 9 10 8 6 4 2

Vintage
20 Vauxhall Bridge Road,
London SW1V 2SA

Vintage is part of the Penguin Random House group of companies whose addresses can be found at global.penguinrandomhouse.com

First published in Vintage in 2018
First published in hardback by Chatto & Windus in 2017

penguin.co.uk/vintage

A CIP catalogue record for this book is available from the British Library

ISBN 9780099592945

Printed and bound by Clays Ltd, St Ives Plc

Penguin Random House is committed to a sustainable future for our business, our readers and our planet. This book is made from Forest Stewardship Council® certified paper.

CONTENTS

List of Illustrations

First Plate Section

Second Plate Section

Every effort has been made to trace or contact copyright holders. The publishers will be pleased to make good any omissions or rectify any mistakes brought to their attention, at the earliest opportunity.

SAPHO LESBIENNE POETRICE.

Chap. 27.

1

What's in a name?

The love that dares not speak its name has never stopped talking. If it was once '*peccatum illud horribile, inter christianos non nominandum*' – that horrible crime not to be named among Christians – it has since been endlessly discussed.

'Queer' was once a term signifying disgust, but now it is pronounced with a difference. It has become the academic word of choice, and 'queer studies' are part of the university curriculum.

'Gay' comes from who knows where. It can be construed as a derivation from '*gai*' in Old Provençal, meaning merry or vivacious, or from '*gaheis*' in Gothic, meaning impetuous, or from '*gahi*' in Frankish, meaning fast. Whatever the language, it used to connote frantic fun and high spirits. In English, 'gay' was originally attached to female prostitutes and the men who chased them. All the gay ladies were on the market. Its twentieth-century same-sex sense seems to have been invented by Americans in the 1940s. There was a long period of incubation before it made its way to England; even in the late 1960s, there were still many who did not understand the phrase 'gay bar'.

Sodomy was, from the eleventh century, a catch-all term that could mean anything or everything. It was applied to heretics and adulterers, blasphemers and idolaters and rebels – anyone, in other words, who disturbed the sacred order of the world. It was also associated with luxury and with pride, and was regularly connected with excessive wealth. It was of course also employed for those who had different ideas about the nature of sexual desire, and was sometimes thrown in as a further accusation with other crimes including buggery.

The 'bugger' was originally a heretic, specifically one of the Albigensian creed which had come from Bulgaria; but since part of that creed condemned matrimonial intercourse, and indeed any kind of natural coupling, the connotations of the word spread beyond the grounds of religion. It is derived from the French *bougre*, as in *pauvre bougre* or poor sod.

The 'ingle', or depraved boy, was well known by the end of the sixteenth century. Is there a phrase – every nook should have an ingle? Ingal Road still survives in east London. 'Pathic', or the passive partner, came to the light of day in the early seventeenth century; ironically the pathic did not need to be aroused, but the male agent did. Yet only the pathic was punished. It was a question of social, rather than sexual, disfavour. The pathic was following his own path in defiance of convention and in dereliction of his social duty. He was like a cat among sheep.

'Catamite' was coined in the same period as pathic. A 'chicken' was an underage boy, hence the term 'chicken hawk'. Such words might have had an underground existence for many decades before becoming common currency since, of course, the activity was still not to be named. The prototype of slang terms for all boy queers was the young and beardless 'Ganymede', often portrayed with a cockerel in his hand and also known as *kinaidos*.

In the eighteenth century 'mollies' were singled out for attention. 'Jemmy' was an abbreviation for James I whose appetites were well known, although a less common term was 'indorsers' from the boxing slang for pummelling the back of an opponent.

In one Newgate transcript a pickpocket is advised to 'leave these *Indorsers* to their beastly Appetites'. A more polite term was 'fribble' after a character invented by David Garrick. Other eighteenth-century terms included 'madge' and 'windward passage' as well as 'caudlemaking' or 'giving caudle' from the Latin *cauda* for tail. Queers were often called 'backgammon players' or 'gentlemen of the back door', sometimes engaged in 'caterwauling'. They might also engage in 'gamahuche', or the act of fellatio, which was applied to females as well as males.

Effeminacy has always been part of what David Garrick, as Mr Fribble, called 'ooman nater'. It was not entirely reserved for queers, and indeed was also applied to men who loved women too dearly for their own good. In John Wycliffe's biblical translation of the late fourteenth century, '*effeminati*' is rendered as 'men maad wymmenysch'. They were considered self-indulgent and silly. They were soft or weak. To complicate matters still further, they may have been asexual.

'Effeminate' is not to be confused with 'camp' which implies a deliberate intention to divert, to shock, or to amuse; camp suggests a flourish, or a display, and it is supposed to come from the Italian verb *campeggiare*, to stand out or to dominate. The sovereign of camp was, perhaps, the 'queen' or 'quean'. The word was first applied to immodest or bold women, the strong ones of their sex, but by the early twentieth century it was equally applied to extravagant queers who could out-female the females.

A Hungarian, Karl-Maria Benkert, coined the term '*homo-szexualitás*' in 1869, thus becoming one of the unacknowledged legislators of mankind. It was for him not a question of morality, but of classification. The subject needed a clinician rather than a priest. Flowers are still placed on Benkert's grave. Twenty-three years later, Charles Gilbert Chaddock rendered his term into English where it has remained ever since. Havelock Ellis described it as a 'barbarous neologism, sprung from a monstrous mingling of Greek and Latin stock' but he may have been mistaking the word for the deed.

When in 1918 J. R. Ackerley was asked whether he was 'homo or hetero', he did not know what the question meant. Another English memoirist, T. C. Worsley, recalled that in 1929 homosexuality 'was still a technical term, the implications of which I was not entirely aware of'. Even in the 1950s elderly gentlemen were flummoxed by the word. It did not arrive in the Valhalla of the *Oxford English Dictionary* until the supplement of 1976.

Another term emerged in 1862, in the work of Karl Heinrich Ulrichs. 'Uranian' or 'urning' was derived from Plato's description of same-sex love in the *Symposium* as '*ouranios*' or 'heavenly'. ('*Ouranos*' literally means 'the pisser', opening up a further line of enquiry.) Whatever its celestial origins, the term did not quite catch on. Who would want to be called an 'urning'? It sounds like some sort of gnome. An 'urnind' was a queer female, while 'uranodionings' were bisexual. Further awkward nomenclatures were found, 'similisexualism' and 'homogenic love' among them. The 'invert' was also discovered in the late nineteenth century, but he did not prosper as much as 'pervert'.

Various euphemisms were in use among the mixed band of brothers and sisters in the late nineteenth century. Is he *earnest*? Is he *so*? Is he *musical*? Is he *theatrical*? Is he *temperamental*? Is he *TBH*? Or, in other words, is he *to be had*? A pair of young men, in the 1930s, might be asked whether they '*share a flat*'. Less euphemistic terms included 'fairy', 'shirt-lifter', 'pansy', 'nancy boy', 'pervert', 'bone-smoker', 'poof' which had once been 'puff', 'sissy', 'Mary Anne', 'fudge-packer', 'butt-piler', 'pillow biter' and, in the American tongue, 'faggot' or 'fag'.

Faggots were the sticks of wood on top of which accused sodomites were burned to death. That is, at least, one explanation. It may equally derive from the schoolboy drudge of a senior prefect. More complicated words came out of thin air. A 'dangler', in the nineteenth century, was one who pretended to like women but in reality did not.

The female variants of same-sex passion included 'sapphist' and 'lesbian' after the peerless poet of Lesbos, the latter term first appearing in the 1730s. 'Sapphist' often became 'sapph' in the early twentieth century. There are also allusions to 'tribades' or 'tribadic women' that come from both Latin and Greek sources. There is the 'fricatrice', one who rubs, and 'subigatrice', one who works a furrow. A 'tommy' is to be found in eighteenth-century England, and is first mentioned in the *Sapphic Epistle* of 1777. 'Butch', 'femme', 'dyke', 'bull-dyke' and 'diesel-dyke' can still sometimes be heard.

The use of the word 'queer' signifies defiance and a refusal to use Karl-Maria Benkert's clinical neologism – homosexuality. 'Queer' can also be construed as being beyond gender. It is an accommodating term, and will be used as such in this study. But it does not preclude the use of other words in this volume, such as gay, where they seem to be more appropriately or more comfortably placed. 'Homoerotic', another refugee from the twentieth century, may be useful in an emergency. It might also be necessary to invoke 'LGBTQIA', beginning with lesbian and ending with asexuality with transgender somewhere in the middle.

So queer people stream out of space and time, each with his or her own story of difference. Some may consider this to be a queer narrative, therefore, but the queerer the better.

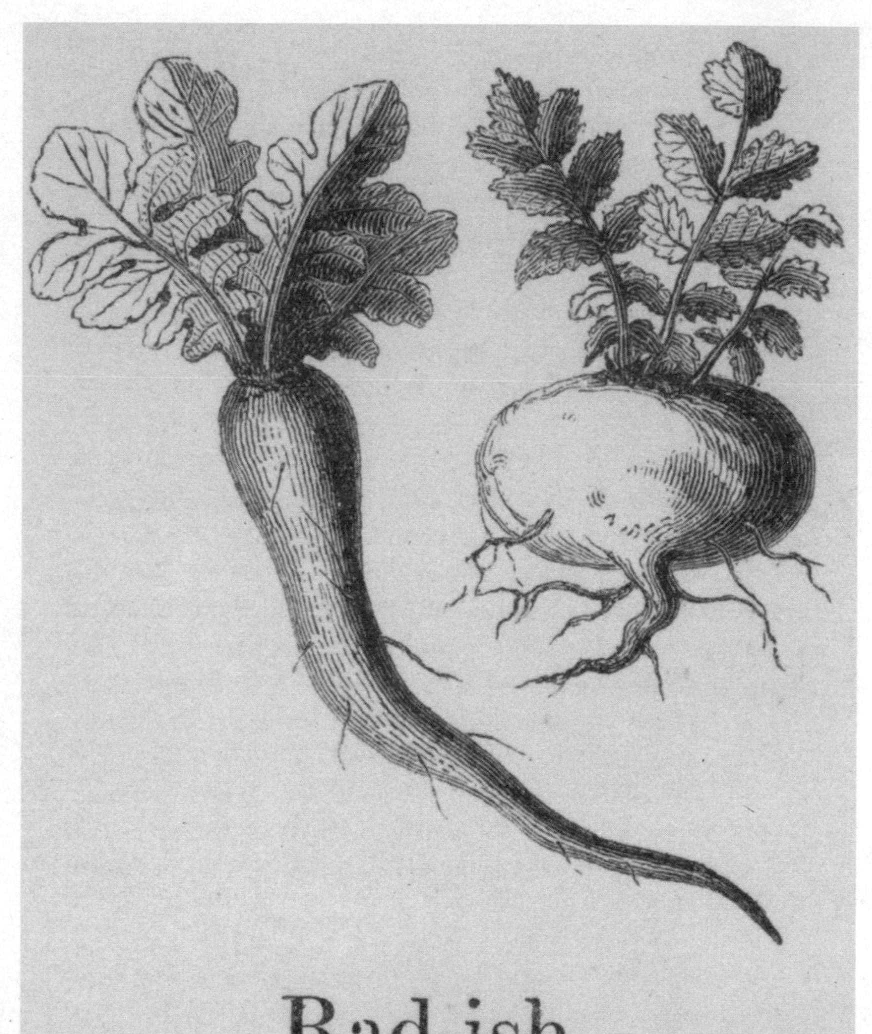

Rad-ish.

2

A red and savage tongue

Of London, before the Romans came, little has been recorded. Yet it may be possible to peer into the supposititious Celtic twilight in order to glimpse unfamiliar passions. The name of the city itself is presumed to be of Celtic origin. It is easy to imagine that the male members of these early tribes were avowedly active in manner and nature, tearing out the heart of a stag with one hand while beating the taut animal skin of a drum with the other. In fact many of their leaders dressed in female clothes and, in ritual ceremonial, imitated the female orgasm and the pains of labour. Aristotle observed that the Celts 'openly held in honour passionate friendship between men'; he uses the Greek word *synousia* for that passion, literally meaning 'being together with' or 'of the same nature as', but in more vulgar terms alluding to sexual intercourse. The Celts were known for their dark complexions and dark, curly hair. Oil was the lubricant of choice. 'They wear their hair long,' Julius Caesar wrote, 'and shave all their bodies with the exception of their heads and their upper lips.' You can still see them walking in the streets of London.

Strabo, the Greek philosopher and geographer, declared that Celtic youths were 'prodigal of their youthful charms'. His near contemporary, Diodorus Siculus, commented in his universal history that the Celts paid little attention to their women but were instead greedy for male embraces; he recorded that it was considered to be a disgrace or a dishonour if a Celtic youth rejected an adult male's sexual advances. The men lay on animal skins with a young male bed-mate on either side. His observation is repeated in Athenaeus of Naucratis, but he may just have been passing on a sexy story which could be applied to the Germanic as well as the Celtic peoples. It may be better to investigate individual tribes, many of them dating to the Mesolithic period, rather than denominate 'Celtic' or 'Germanic' peoples, but the subject is thoroughly confused. We can only speculate on activities rather than origins.

In the fourth century, Eusebius of Caesarea noted that among the tribes young men were ready and eager to marry one another according to custom. Bardesanes of Edessa wrote that 'handsome young men assume the role of wives towards other men, and they celebrate marriage feasts'. Sextus Empiricus wrote of the Germanic people that sodomy was 'not looked upon as shameful but as a customary thing'. The sources, fortunately, all agree.

These handsome young men were not unusual in a predominantly military culture, and the references are so frequent that they suggest an identifiable part of the population who took on the passive role as part of their transition to adulthood. Slaves, the clergy, and those who did not aspire to military honour were also of their number. From the evidence of the scholars, therefore, an alternative to conventional procreation was readily available and much in demand. This has remained throughout the history of London.

In Roman London we are on well-documented foundations. When the conquerors brought their brick and marble, they also brought their social customs. In the beginning two principal streets of gravel ran parallel to the river on the eastern hill. A military camp was established in the north-western quarter of the city. Taverns and brothels grew around them as naturally as wild grass. London was at this time a relatively new settlement, and therefore more receptive or more vulnerable to new practices and influences. By the time it had become a city, and a capital, it had grown out of all proportion. It also had become a rich city, filled with merchants and businessmen (or *negotiatores*) who no doubt purchased bodies as well as goods. It is one of the few settlements on earth that began as a city and has always remained one, with all the commercial and financial entanglements this history implies.

Urban life was conducted in the Roman fashion. The most ubiquitous practice of same-sex love occurred in the relationship between master and slave or between man and boy. The passive partner, in other words, had no political role. In what was essentially a city state, with its own independent government, the difference in status is important. Only the active could rule. Sexuality is not a free agent in society; society defines and dominates sexuality. Warriors who had been overcome in battle could be raped by Roman citizens. The defeated were sometimes instead penetrated by 'radishes'; that may not sound too painful an ordeal but in fact the 'long white icicle radish' has always been grown in southern England to a length of just under six inches.

Paedophilia, or sex with a child, and pederasty, sex with an adolescent, were not condemned. The love between two free men was, on the other hand, considered undesirable and worthy of censure; this is not to say, of course, that it did not happen. But if a man were accused of such *infamia*, he might be stripped of his civic rights.

In the middle of a busy city such as Londinium, many opportunities were afforded by the various *lupanaria* or 'wolf dens' (public pleasure houses), *fornices* (brothels) and the *thermiae* (hot baths). The pleasure houses were expensive, and were no doubt largely patronised by the Roman administrators and Romano-British nobility. The brothels of a lower class might have curtained entrances, behind which a number of small booths were established. The wooden houses had roofs of thatch and brightly painted plaster interiors. The *palaestrae*, or sporting facilities, within the hot baths were well known for casual pickups.

But sex could be advertised in the open, for the delectation of passing trade. Sometimes a male prostitute might stand in front of his own stall or 'cell' waiting for custom. He might also haunt a tavern, a lodging house or a bakery. He might come from the lower classes, or he may have been a foreigner or a slave. Slaves or captured foreigners were disembarked in open spaces near the major quays known as 'Romelands', and may have been sold on the spot; 'Romelands' could be found at Dowgate, Queenhithe, Billingsgate and the Tower. Male prostitutes were prized for the tax raised from them, and they had their own public holiday.

A Roman apologist for Christianity, Minucius Felix, stated that homosexuality was 'the Roman religion' and the second century Assyrian scholar, Tatian, confirmed that pederasty 'was held in pre-eminent esteem by the Romans'. It was considered to be an admirable activity, and was no doubt as common in London as in Rome. It hardly deserved notice or comment, no more than the 'Herms' or stone pillars which stood at the major intersections; they represented Hermes with an erect phallus, and sometimes the phallus alone. It has not been emphasised enough, perhaps due to the modesty of classicists, that Roman society was intensely phallocratic; the worship of the penis was only ever equalled in regions of India.

The queer man in Greek history, who bears some relation to his Roman or even English brother, was described in the anonymous *Physiognomonics* (*c.*300 BC) as having 'an unsteady eye and knock-knees; he inclined his head to the right; he gestures with his palms up and his wrists loose; and he has two styles of walking – either waggling his hips or keeping them under control. He tends to look around in all directions.' He was also *homo delicatus* in Rome and London who, according to Scipio in 129 BC, 'daily perfumes himself and dresses before a mirror, whose eyebrows are trimmed, who walks abroad with beard plucked out and thighs made smooth'. He was soft, with mincing steps and shrill or lisping voice. He wore violet and purple rather than white, but he also loved light green and sky blue. He kept his hand upon his hip and scratched his head with one finger. In his discussion of Britain in his life of Agricola, Tacitus in the first century states that 'the barbarians, as well, learn to condone seductive vices'. He also explains that the Romano-British soon imitated the vices and follies of their masters; in their ignorance they called it 'civilisation' but it was really 'a part of their servitude'. New London became the mirror of old Rome.

Sartorial tokens of effeminacy were recorded in some detail by classical authors; you were what you wore. A mantle, made of soft wool, was worn by both sexes but for males had singular connotations. Boots of white leather, reaching to the knee or shin, were another sign. Garments dyed with saffron were worn by men with a difference. An 'oriental' headdress, resembling a turban, was considered effeminate as was a 'soft shoe' designed for wearing indoors. A sandal fastened to the sole by leather straps was deemed to be inappropriate, as were fine shawls or veils. Long and loose clothing, including the ankle-length tunic and the unbelted tunic, were not considered sufficiently male. Tattooing was also suspect. It used to be believed that graves containing jewellery were those of females, but that convenient illusion has been dispelled. It is now clear that men wore earrings, finger rings, or neck rings (torcs). An image of Harpocrates has been found in London; it is of a nubile boy god wearing a gold body chain, a device only previously displayed on goddesses.

Yet the men are only half of it. Some classical scholars have uncovered legal allusions to women lying together or even engaged in permanent or temporary relationships. To the evidence of the antiquarian can be added the discoveries of the archaeologist. In Great Dover Street have been found the remains of a female gladiator. This was within the Southwark district where social outcasts found their last resting place. She was in her early twenties. One of the objects buried with her was a lamp showing a fallen gladiator. The grave goods included stone pines (*pinus pinea*) which have only ever been found in the great amphitheatre of Roman London where they disguised the noxious smells.

She seems to have attracted wealthy admirers, despite her status as an outcast, and may be evidence of the popular fervour attached to the more daring contestants. Other female gladiators in the classical world are recorded with their own habits and customs. Many allusions were made to them and contests were sometimes held between women and dwarves. A marble relief, now in the British Museum, shows two women armed for combat.

Their sexuality, if such it was, can only be surmised. 'How can a woman be decent,' Juvenal wrote, 'sticking her head in a helmet, denying the sex she was born with?' There may be a further connection with London. Petronius writes of a female *essedaria*, a gladiatress, fighting from a British chariot. This is decidedly odd. Classical sources tell us also that in England women were as tall and strong as the men. Two females, in their mid-twenties, were found curled together in a burial site beneath Rangoon Street in the City of London. They were relatively sturdy with strong legs and feet; it is possible that they were accustomed to carrying heavy loads in building work or some other trade. Another joint female burial is recorded on the bank of the Thames at Bull Ward; one of them was older and had been killed with a blow to her skull. Beside her was a much younger and smaller woman, with a height of four feet and nine inches. They may have been sisters, but they may not.

It is pertinent to note that male gladiators often gave themselves effeminate names such as Hyacinthus and Narcissus, and it seems more than likely that they had as many male as female admirers. They dressed to kill, with tunics made up of tassels and threads of gold, and with elaborate armbands. Inscriptions set up in their honour have plausibly homoerotic explanations. They sometimes conducted tours of England like a band of thespians. Many statues and copper lamps and bowls, and even earrings, displaying Hercules are found in London; characteristically he is nude and beardless, with short and straight 'Celtic' hair; he holds his club in his right hand but, in a find at Walbrook, three cupids hold up this weapon. He was in any case a divine hero for some Londoners.

But divinity assumed another face. In the early fourth century the shadow of the cross fell upon Londinium. The change to Christian faith may not have been immediate but it was far-reaching. The bishops and their clergy came. The monks came. The missionaries continued to come. This was the century when the first laws were enacted against certain queer practices, although full prohibition of homosexuality was not enjoined until the sixth century.

As the cities of the Roman Empire declined, greater animus was directed against any and all minorities that had flourished in an urban setting. In the reign of the Byzantine emperor of the sixth century, Justinian, the sentence for sodomitical activity was castration of both parties, which in effect was a sentence of death. One law, promulgated in 538, warned the people of Constantinople that homosexual acts would 'incur the just anger of God, and bring about the destruction of cities along with their inhabitants'. The example of Rome could be adduced but so might the decay of Londinium which had been left undefended by the early fifth century.

The earliest arrival of the Saxons has been dated to the beginning of the same century. According to the historian Gildas, the inhabitants of England were licked by a 'red and savage tongue'. The archaeological evidence suggests that the city was thoroughly Saxonised by the middle of the sixth century, and Lundenwic emerged in what is now Covent Garden.

The Anglo-Saxons – essentially a collection of Jutes, Angles, Frisians and Saxons who had arrived at different times and in different regions – had not yet been recruited for Christianity and they maintained their indigenous sexual traditions. The Roman descriptions of their homosexual propensities are so similar to accounts of the Celtic and the Germanic tribes that for all practical effects they are indistinguishable. It is of course true that there are limits to what two men can do to, or with, one another. And it is also true that early historians often simply copied what they had read elsewhere.

It was a world of warriors governed by a rich and intense male culture. The young men of the noble class wore linen tunics, fastened at the wrist and waist by golden clasps; their clothes were ornamented with brooches and other jewels. Men as well as women dyed their hair; blue, green and orange were the colours favoured by the men. The early histories have their own salacious legends. When Mempricius, the fifth king of the Britons, turned to sodomy he was devoured by wolves. When

Malgo, a sixth-century king of the Saxons, indulged in sodomy or 'a sinne against kynde' he died suddenly in his bath at the palace of Winchester.

The earliest collections of Anglo-Saxon laws make no mention of same-sex activity; the oldest code, from Ethelbert of Kent in the early seventh century, punishes bestiality, rape, adultery and incest but does not even allude to homosexuality. In the ninth century, Alfred quotes the Bible on the punishment of death for men who have sex with sheep but lays down no penalty at all for men who have sex with men. The dog never barks.

Saxon men were taller and heavier than the Romans or the Celts; they were clean-shaven but often sported bushy moustaches. Many had short hair in the belief that cropped hair rendered their faces larger and therefore fiercer. They may not have varied greatly from the Angles and Jutes who had crossed the sea with them, but were they prettier when younger? Bede recounts how Pope Gregory saw some young Angles on sale in a market of Rome, with 'fair complexions, fine-cut features and beautiful hair'. The Pope is supposed to have said: '*Non Angli, sed angeli*'; but the little angels were no doubt destined for a fate harsher than a heavenly choir. The remark was later held against Gregory on the grounds that he was also a sodomite. As he might have said, '*Vincere non potest.*' You can't win.

Christianity did not arrive formally in England until 597 when Augustine landed at Thanet to convert the Germanic, rather than the British, people. Soon enough the Church had become an instrument of government and the Christian penitentials offered stern guidance for the punishment of sin. Homosexuality may not have been mentioned in the Anglo-Saxon codes but in Christian documents it took an important role. In the penitentials the punishment for fornicating with another man was a penance of four years, and of ten or fifteen years for a further offence; a penance of seven years was applied to a 'sodomita' or 'mollis' for his general bearing in the world. It is clear enough that there was already a specific and recognisable group or community of queers which were given especial names by the larger society. One such name was *baedling*, which is derived from the Anglo-Saxon word for a boy or an effeminate man. It can also be interpreted as one who spends too much time in bathhouses. It has been suggested by some scholars that 'bad' derives from *baedling*, thus giving universal moral significance to a sexual difference. In a similar spirit of queer etymological conjecture, it has been surmised that 'felon' comes from *fellare*, to suck.

From another code (*c.*670s), associated with Theodore, Archbishop of Canterbury, comes the injunction that 'If boys fornicate between themselves he judged that they are to be beaten'. It is also laid down that 'who releases semen into the mouth, seven years of penance; this is the worst evil'. A boy who engages in intercourse with an adult male in holy orders is to fast for three periods of forty days. No punishment is assigned to the man. The boy was considered to be the temptor and instigator, perhaps, and it was a way of preserving authority in a male environment; it may also be that the period of fasting was a way of removing pollution from the child. Yet if it seems manifestly unjust it serves to emphasise the difference between early medieval and modern sexuality. One section of a penitential has a ringing introduction. 'Let us Now Set Forth the Decree of Our Fathers before Us on the Sinful Playing of Boys.'

Another British penitential, compiled by Vinnian, also mentions fellatio. 'Those who satisfy their desires with their lips, three years. If it has become a habit, seven years.' He also denounces '*in terga fornicantes*', having sex through the back, but leaves the punishment to the discretion of the priest-confessor. It is clear enough, however, that at no time did the canons of Christian law evince the slightest tolerance for same-sex love. It was always forbidden, even though it did not become a capital offence until the sixteenth century.

The presence of same-sex love among women is noticed in the penitentials as well. 'If a woman has intercourse with another woman, she is to fast three years.' Another penitential discusses the use of a *machina* or instrument, which sounds very much like a dildo. Transvestism by either male or female is not considered a sexual offence but is regarded as an aspect of witchcraft or some other pagan practice. It is not uncommon for a male corpse to be buried alongside grave goods normally associated with females, a phenomenon that has prompted some archaeologists to contemplate the existence of a 'third gender' among the Anglo-Saxons. This would correspond with evidence from other parts of the world, from the *berdaches* of Dakota to the Bhoota dancers of South India. The questions of why and when this sexual diversity was restrained or eliminated, if in fact it ever was, are part of the story of the queer city.

If men can be of ambiguous gender, so can women. There are many stories of religious women or holy women who dressed, worked and lived like men. They cut their hair, one of the prime tokens of femality. They might dress as monks in order to emphasise their double vocation. They have renounced their nature for service to God. Some of them were not discovered to be women until the time of their death.

Another Anglo-Saxon penitential refers to a married man who enjoys having sex with male partners, and an aggressive male known as *waepnedman* (*waepned* with connotations of arms or armour) who has intercourse with similarly masculine men. We might say, therefore, that some of the characteristics of modern gay life are to be found in the first and second-century city. Terms such as *baedling* or *mollis* also indicate some kind of permanent sexual identity, part of a passive subculture that may have flourished in Anglo-Saxon London despite the strictures of the Church. The connotations and explanations, however, were different from those of the twenty-first century. The participants may or may not have been 'queer' but no one could tell. The matter is irrelevant. The word and concept were unknown.

In some penitentials the punishments were relatively mild. Women were obliged to do penance of 160 days for same-sex love, and males incurred a year of fasting and prayer. But it was not condign punishment. A priest who went hunting, for example, was consigned to three years of penitence. It seems likely that same-sex activity was considered no more or less reprehensible than sex outside marriage. It was certainly favoured by the clergy. They may have taken their inspiration from the paired military saints, such as Juventin and Maximin, where fraternal love peeks over the borders of same-sex love. They may have been encouraged in England itself where, according to St Boniface in 744, the people were 'lusting after the fashion of the people of Sodom'. One English cleric of the period, Alcuin, more associated with York rather than London, is very effusive in one letter to another man; he wants to lick his breast, and kiss his fingers and his toes. It has been suggested that this is part of an epistolary tradition but the language is so vivid that it is hard to know where custom ends and private passion begins. As C. S. Lewis remarked in *The Allegory of Love* (1936), 'the deepest worldly emotion in this period is the love of man for man'.

This was also the characteristic of the various invaders who conquered and occupied London over succeeding centuries, among them the Vikings and the Normans. Two Old Norse words, 'ergi' and 'argr', expressed dark or angry hints of homoeroticism and communal betrayal. Norse words existed for active as well as passive roles in same-sex intercourse although, curiously enough, the person who made the original accusation of sodomy was in danger of outlawry or even death. There was no penalty for the incident itself. The Vikings, having the sea in their blood, may have had that sexual insouciance which is supposedly characteristic of sailors. Their sagas abound in references to *koerleikr*, which can be construed as love between men.

A medical compendium of the early eleventh century described 'a disease which befalls a man who is accustomed to have other men lie on him. He has great sexual desire, and a great deal of sperm, which is not moved.' It goes on to counsel 'the men who try to cure these people' that 'their illness lies in their imagination. It is not natural. The only cure is to break their desire through sadness, hunger, sleeplessness, imprisonment and flogging.' It is another example that sexual passivity was considered to be more troubling and disruptive than sexual activity. 'Sadness' can be interpreted as seriousness or gravity; the queers were guilty, among much else, of frivolity.

By the twelfth century same-sex love came to be considered as the prevailing vice of Norman nobles, princes and kings. How could it not be so in a military caste that relied upon masculine loyalty and friendship? The Normans were in fact notorious for their sexual preference. Willing boys were no doubt to be found by the military fortifications of Montfichet Tower, Baynard's Castle and the south-east section of the Wall that later became known as the Tower.

William I, or 'Conqueror', was not of their number; but his son, William II or William Rufus, was inclined to the practices of Sodom. He never married and had no children, a startling circumstance for a king. Even those who disliked their wives usually did their duty and continued the line. Instead he surrounded himself with what the chroniclers call 'effeminates' with mincing step and loose or extravagant clothing. His friends loved soft clothes and soft bedding. They wore tight shirts and tunics. They wore shoes with pointed toes. They wore their long hair loose, with ringlets that tumbled down to the shoulders and were sometimes decorated with ribbons; crisping irons were in regular use, as they were in the later reign of John. The English historian William of Malmesbury commented that the youths were often naked and competed with each other for the softness of their skin; they 'break their step with a licentious gesture'. It was said that at night the lamps of the court were extinguished so that sexual sins might be committed under the cover of darkness. Yet an alternative explanation is possible. The young men were called 'effeminate' because they loved women too much. That was one of the meanings of the word. It has been proposed that the allusions to homosexuality were really part of the propaganda against the Norman overseers. This proviso must always be kept in mind.

Nevertheless it was widely considered to set an unfortunate example to the subjects of the king, and it was constantly assailed by the more vigorous or courageous Anglo-Norman clerics. Anselm, who became Archbishop of Canterbury in 1093, preached against the male tradition of long hair at court and requested that William II should convene a conference on the evils of his reign, particularly 'the most shameful crime of sodomy'. The king ordered his archbishop never to mention the matter again. It made no difference in any case. Anselm's biographer, Eadmer, mentions that long hair became so much the fashion that short-haired courtiers were known as 'country bumpkins' or even 'priests'. A question was asked: 'If you don't do what courtiers do, what are you doing in court?'

It was said that, after the Normans came, homosexuality spread in England like syrup through water. It was largely considered to be an urban phenomenon and certain London monasteries, such as those in Bermondsey, Aldgate, Clerkenwell, Shoreditch, Cornhill, Holborn and Cripplegate, were not immune. The abbot of Rievaulx, even in far-off Yorkshire, allowed his monks to hold hands as a mark of their affection. It was based on the model of Jonathan's intense love for David 'passing the love of women'. Would it have been worse in London itself, at the centre of insatiable sin? An eleventh-century manuscript shows a group of sodomites, huddled together, staring intently at each other. William Rufus established a number of monasteries in London where young men and boys mingled. Sodomy may not have been their purpose, but sodomy was the effect. We come across the name of one Robert Badding which, from its association with *baedling*, implies that he was an effeminate man. There were many others.

The jokes and innuendoes, concerning 'foul catamites', 'loathsome Ganymedes', 'effeminates' and 'sodomite-things' are in any case extant. The worst was always to be assumed. Monks and their entourage of pupils or novices were open to remark in the public streets. St Bernard of Clairvaux took a crippled boy to bed. It was supposed to elicit a miracle but did not. The chronicler, Walter Map, remarked that 'he was then the most unlucky of monks, for I have heard before now of a monk throwing himself upon a boy, but always, when the man rose up, the boy rose up too'. It was universally agreed that monks did it. Indeed there was probably something wrong with them if they did not. When relationships between the same sex happen to fit a particular social unit or social institution, the results will be obvious.

In 1120 a ship bearing the only son and heir of Henry I, William Adeline, perished on some rocks between France and England with only two survivors. The cause of the shipwreck was generally assigned to the number of court sodomites on board.

PREMIERS TEMPLIERS,

EN HABIT DE GUERRE A CHEVAL,

Figures 10 et 11.

3

A military lay

In 1102 a Church council met in solemn conclave in London, confirming the status of the capital as one of the great cities of the Holy Roman Empire. William Rufus had been dead two years and Archbishop Anselm now pressed the case against sodomy he had been pursuing for most of his career. It was the central concern of the conference, all the more pertinent in a city where the activity was prevalent. An edict was drawn up condemning 'the shameful sin of sodomy', but very little seems to have been done about it. Anselm himself confessed 'this sin has hitherto been so public that hardly anyone is embarrassed by it, and many have therefore fallen into it because they were unaware of its seriousness'. It was reported by Roger of Chester, however, that 'eight abbots, with a great crew of inferior priests and friars, were found guilty'. One feature of early medieval life is the passing of strong edicts and the threats of serious punishments as a way of avoiding any action at all. Fines were more convenient. Henry I, the new king, probably needed all the money he could mulct from the clergy for their abominable vices. There does seem to have been a supplementary desire to cut long hair from the heads of men and to cut beards from those 'bearded like goats or Saracens' but, of its nature, the persecution did not endure.

It could not have withstood the opposition of the knights who gathered around a succeeding king. The funereal effigy of Richard I at Fontevraud Abbey shows him with flowing hair and a full beard. He, too, has over the centuries been accused of queer proclivities. He often berated himself for what he called, obliquely, 'that sin'. While Duke of Aquitaine he engaged in a close friendship with Philip, King of France, to the extent that his father, Henry II, 'was absolutely astonished at the passionate love between them and marvelled at it'. No bed separated them. Yet it may have been merely a political gesture. Why else would you sleep with a king? He was also supposed to be interested in Raife de Clermon, a young knight whom he rescued from captivity.

The bonds between military men in a feudal state are always open to question, of course. The companionship of knights seems to know no bounds, and the mutual gaze between them can be interpreted as a form of touch. In the Anglo-Norman military lay 'Sir Launfal', the hero is told that 'you have no desire for women. You have well trained young men and enjoy yourself with them.' If you live, eat, sleep and hunt together what else might you do? The love between men was the basis of the feudal ties between warriors. The *chansons* and *lais* were written to celebrate the love of comrades, or of an older for a younger man. Boys over the age of seven were considered to be susceptible to 'the sin against kind'. Many of the sagas attend exclusively to the homosocial bond. Layamon's *Brut*, the metrical chronicle of England begun in the late twelfth century, states that in court 'men loved men' – '*wapmon luuede wapmon*' – and despised women.

Bands of noble youths might endure for twenty years, spending every moment in the company of one another. When a group of companions left their household in Cester or Chester they returned, according to Ordericus Vitalis, '*quasi di flammis Sodomiae*', as if from the flames of Sodom. Thomas Malory recalls the presence of transvestite knights in chivalric contests. It was an old tradition, evoking the tournament as a play world in which sex is ambiguous. This was also the period when 'Hilary the

Englishman' composed his poems in honour of the beauty of boys, two of them to English boys of sweet flesh and golden hair, who duplicated the roles of cup-bearer or bedfellow. An English cleric, John of Salisbury, describes with some interest the gestures of a 'wanton' who begins to stroke and caress the hands and legs of a desired one. 'Growing bolder he allows his hand to pass over the entire body with lecherous caress, incites the lascivious thrill he has aroused, and fans the flames of languishing desire.'

London itself had evolved vigorously and rapidly, with all the attendant problems of overpopulation, poverty and disease; greater sexual freedom was an inevitable consequence. Men of sodomitical persuasion were said to be 'as numerous as grains of barley, as many as the shells of the sea, or the sands of the shore'. Richard of Devizes, a late-twelfth-century chronicler, described how 'all sorts of men crowd together there from every country under the heavens . . . every quarter of it abounds in great obscenities' and among them were *glabriones* (smooth-skinned, pretty boys), *pusiones* (hustlers), *molles* (effeminates) and *mascularii* (man lovers). It could be a picture of London over the centuries.

We cannot at this late date take off the roofs of the houses, in the literary conceit of the period, but we can see the life of the city from a distance. Male servants generally slept together. Male guests in a hostel or inn were expected to sleep together, generally naked. The head of the household would have every opportunity to indulge his tastes. An unmarried master and his apprentice might share a rudimentary bed. The beds were everywhere in the house, and the concept of privacy did not exist. It was a public and intensely social world.

Schoolmasters paid as much attention to the buttocks as the brains of their little pupils. Everyone knew, or was told, that the aristocrats and the senior clergy were engaged with their own sex all the time. Undergraduates at the two universities slept together, if only to keep warm. Public baths on the model of the Turkish *hammam* were established with all the refinements which the Eastern world knew. This was one of the more sybaritic legacies of the Crusades.

The recesses of London Bridge, erected in 1209, were used for other purposes as well as public latrines. A case of 1306 reveals that a plaintiff asked his servant to follow the defendant, 'the which he did through diverse streets until they came to London Bridge where he [the defendant] told the servant to wait for him while he went to the privy there . . . and then left the privy by another entrance'. So there was room for assignations and sudden departures. By the Thames at Queenhithe a 'necessary house' was greatly enlarged in 1237, and no doubt attracted the usual clients or customers.

Some charges of 1339 outline the contours of queer London in the packed and dirty streets of Holborn, the Fleet, Chancery Lane and Shoe Lane. Gilbert le Strengmaker, of the Hospital Rents in Fleet Street, was accused of harbouring 'men of ill fame' in what seems to have been a brothel. Agnes and Juliana, two sisters from Holborn, were accused of the same crime. Suspect houses were mentioned in Chancery Lane, Fetter Lane, Shoe Lane and Hosier Lane. It may be that the men of ill fame were commonplace thieves or robbers, but the context suggests another explanation.

The strange denunciations and counter-accusations of the Lombards, the Knights Templar, and others, heightened the atmosphere. When Peter Pateshull preached against the Augustinians in the pulpit of St Christopher's, London, in 1387, his Lollard followers attacked the friars with the cry '*Incendamus sodomitas*'. Let us burn these sodomites! The Lollards nailed up the 'Twelve Conclusions of the Lollards' to the great doors of Westminster Hall during the parliamentary session of 1395 with the stark message that 'the English people bewail the crime of Sodom'. The third 'conclusion' states that sodomy can be the result of overeating delicate foods; sodomites vomit and they have to be purged, which might be seen as an image of sexual horror. It adds that 'the secret test of such men is, that they like no women; and when you prove such a man mark him well, for he is one of those'. Sodomy was also a 'priue synne', a private sin; secrecy was of its essence, just as a heretic might skulk in the shadows. An anonymous verse claims that 'the race of the Lollards is the vile race of Sodom'. The charge was ubiquitous precisely because it was elusive and indefinite.

Many marginal groups were considered, at one stage, to be heretical and therefore capable of sodomy. Some say that one of the directives of the Knights Templar was to go out and sin with one another by way of buggery; others say that they were obliged to copulate as part of their order. This is speculation. It is a matter of record, however, that one Londoner, Robertus le Dorturer, a notary of the city, accused a member of the order of trying to sodomise him. Another London witness, Johannes de Presbur, accused a Templar of trying to have sex with one of his male relatives. These two instances do not make a high summer of sodomy. It is certainly true that the reigning monarch, Edward II, did not fully believe the reports of their activities and avoided bringing the Knights to trial until the last minute. He may have had some sympathy for their plight if not necessarily their tastes. They were burned in Paris, in large quantities, but not in London. The courts at Westminster sent them into exile at Ponthieu, one of Edward's French territories.

The women were not spared attention. The eleventh of the 'Twelve Conclusions of the Lollards' alludes to 'secret sins' of the women of the Church, and that women 'who are fickle and imperfect by nature' are 'the cause of bringing the most horrible sin possible to mankind'. There is no doubt about the nature of the sin. The spiritual guide for the nuns of England in the early thirteenth century, the *Ancrene Riwle*, mentions (although it says that it will *not* mention) 'the scorpion of stynkande Leccherie'. Again the reference to same-sex passion is clear. The phenomenon was perfectly well known as '*mulier cum muliere fornicans*' or '*muliercum muliere fornicationem committens*', which perhaps does not need translation. It was rumoured that women mixed male sperm with their food to make them more manly, and that they frequently fashioned a 'heavy contrivance in the shape of a male member'. It was believed that females were sexually insatiable, and so were inclined to leap into bed with each other. It was not a question of being gay or queer, or whatever word we choose to use, but simply an outpouring of the nature of womankind. It was Eve's sin of lasciviousness or, perhaps, of curiosity.

By the late thirteenth century, however, certain signs of disapproval became more manifest in England. As early as 1250 the Bishop of London, Fulk Bassett, called for the punishment of sodomites. The wrath of the clergy grew fiercer. A legal compilation known as *Britton* declares that the penalty for sodomy was death by fire. A treatise of 1290, *Fleta*, was named after the fact that its author lived in Fleet Street, London. It stated that a convicted sodomite should be buried alive. Every sort of explanation has been offered for this apparent sea change in judicial policy, from the hegemony of the Church to the threat of the Turks in the East and to the rise of centralised monarchies, but it seems likely that the law was meant to bark rather than bite. No cases of burning or premature burial are recorded in London. The deliciousness of revenge could be relished in texts, however; the *Golden Legend* of 1260 comments that, at the time of the birth of Christ, all sodomites suddenly expired.

PIERS GAVESTON AND THE BARONS.

4

The friend

Piers Gaveston, the younger son of a Gascon knight, entered the service of Edward I in the army at Flanders in 1297 but the king, impressed by the grace and bearing of the young man, soon appointed him to the household of the Prince of Wales. He may have been considered a model of male conduct and deportment from which the prince would learn. Prince Edward seems to have learned other lessons from his new companion, however, and as a result the king sent Gaveston into temporary exile, though the young man was still granted an annuity 'for as long as he shall remain in parts beyond the sea during the king's pleasure and waiting recall'. It would appear that the king wished to keep him apart from his son, perhaps as a punishment to the prince himself.

It has been asserted that the young men were 'sworn brothers' rather than lovers. An anonymous chronicler states that 'when the king's son gazed upon him, he immediately felt so much love for him that he entered into a covenant of brotherhood with him and firmly resolved to bind himself to him, before all mortals, in an unbreakable bond of love'. They became what were known as 'wedded brethren', a union which could in fact be solemnised before the altar. It is one explanation that would address the very florid ties of manhood that characterised the early fourteenth century. But it emphasises the fine, and perhaps non-existent, line between male camaraderie and same-sex love. The chroniclers recall that the relationship between them was 'excessive' and 'immoderate' which suggests that it went beyond the chivalric bond. This was also the charge later raised against Richard II and his 'obscene intimacies' with his favourite, Robert de Vere. These accusations were the occupational hazard of any young king and his companions.

On the death of his father in 1307, Edward II recalled Gaveston and bestowed upon him the earldom of Cornwall as well as other lavish gifts. The two men were inseparable, to the growing alarm of the greater lords, and when Gaveston was appointed *custos regni*, or regent, in anticipation of the departure of the king for France, the dismay of his rivals grew. The Earl of Cornwall's closeness to the king became even more notorious on the occasion of Edward's marriage to Isabella of France; the earl took the lead in the ceremonies, and monopolised the king's attention to such an extent that Isabella's relatives walked out in disgust.

It could only end in tears. In 1308 the great barons of the realm demanded that the favourite go once more into exile, with the implicit threat of civil war if the king declined to order his departure. He was forced to comply but, a month later, he appointed his favourite as king's lieutenant in Ireland. Gaveston returned to England but was once more forced into exile in 1311. He still retained the love of the king, however, and came back at the beginning of 1312. But this was the last time. He was surrounded and arrested by the barons, his head cut off by the Earl of Warwick on 19 June 1312.

This is one of the first instances in the English historical record when a queer relationship between king and courtier has been suggested, or surmised, or hinted at, by the chroniclers. The anonymous author of a life of Edward II, written soon after the events related, added that 'I do not remember to have heard that one man so loved another . . . our king was incapable of moderate favour, and on account of Piers was said to forget himself. And so Piers was accounted a sorcerer.' His audience would have known well enough that sorcery was associated with sodomy. A Cistercian chronicler recorded that Edward II '*in vitio sodomitico nimium delectabat*', or, in other words, that he wallowed in sodomy. This did not of course prevent him from fathering five children, one of them illegitimate; our modern descriptions of what is gay or queer need to be thoroughly revised in order to understand the past.

The Pardoner

5

No cunt

Geoffrey Chaucer provided one of the first portraits, or caricatures, of a London queer. The Pardoner is among the last of the Canterbury pilgrims to be mentioned in Chaucer's human panorama, but he is one of the most distinctive. He has blond hair which he wears long across his shoulders in wisps and locks; this was seen to be the sign of the sodomite. He wears no hood in concordance with the 'the newe jet', or the new fashion. His eyes are shining like those of a hare, another well-known sign of difference. His voice is as high as that of a nanny goat. He has no beard, nor would ever possess one. He is perpetually fair-shaven.

The narrator of *The Canterbury Tales* eventually declares that 'I believe he was a gelding or a mare' – that, literally, he was either a eunuch or a woman. But 'mare' was also used as a term for effeminate men. The Pardoner was one who 'sinned against kind', a 'nurrit', a 'will-jick', in the phrases of the period. The fact that he bartered indulgences and sold false relics only amplified his nature as a 'ful vicious man' and perhaps a heretic as well. He may have also traded other favours. The narrator remarks that 'the somonour bar to hym a stif burdoun'. This might conventionally mean that he furnished the bass harmony for a song but the 'stif burdoun' also has sexual connotations. The narrator notes of the Summoner that 'ful prively a fynch eek koude he pulle' which can imply illicit sexual intercourse with a minor. The Pardoner and the Summoner were, to put it no lower, a couple of reprobates. Out of twenty-three pilgrims only these two are suspected of same-sex love; whether that reflects its general prevalence cannot be known.

At the end of the tale the Pardoner asks the Host to kiss his 'relics', to which comes a thunderous answer:

> 'Let be,' quoth he, 'it shall not be, so the'ch.
> Thou wouldest make me kiss thine olde breech,
> And swear it were a relic of a saint,
> Though it were with thy fundament depaint.
> But, by the cross which that Saint Helen fand,
> I would I had thy coilons in mine hand,
> Instead of relics, or of sanctuary.
> Let cut them off, I will thee help them carry;
> They shall be shrined in a hogge's turd.'
> The Pardoner answered not one word;
> So wroth he was, no worde would he say.

This torrent of words, including 'fundament' and 'breech', 'coilons' (testicles) and 'turd', testifies to the range of associations which even an allusion to being a homosexual can summon forth from the deep. Chaucer apologised for his lapse of taste but pleaded that the Bible itself contains references to sodomy but that the holy text is no more defiled by it 'than the sun that shines on a dunghill'.

In the treatises written in the lifetime of Geoffrey Chaucer, the effeminate man is characterised as fearful and timid, like a hare; he has little body hair, and is deceitful. This could well be the Pardoner who, it has also been suggested, might be a female transvestite and even perhaps a hermaphrodite. This emphasises the fruitful confusion of gender roles in the period. There may have been many individuals who would now be classified as 'transgender', even though such a role or classification was not then available. They suffered the hell of perpetual bewilderment on the earth.

Other poems of the period, written in what has become known as 'Middle English', are witness to the extent of interest in the subject of same-sex intercourse. Passages of *Cleanness* written in the late fourteenth century are devoted to the acts 'contrived against nature' when 'each male takes as his mate a man like himself' and, in the same style as the words of the Host to the Pardoner, the subject elicits allusions to arse, the breech, breeches and intolerable smells. The references here are to anal sex. In *Vision of Piers Plowman* (1370–90) William Langland writes of the period when, after heterosexual intercourse, 'males drowen hem to males'. In a morality play of 1470, *Mankind*, the character of 'New Guise' is portrayed as an effeminate homosexual. 'Alas, master, alas,' he calls out at an awkward moment, 'My privity!' To which Mischief replies, 'Wait! I shall see it all too soon.'

These were not merely literary allusions. Between the hours of eight and nine on a Sunday night, in early December 1394, some London officials picked up a prostitute, John Rykener, 'calling him/herself Eleanor'. He was arrested in Soper Lane, south of Cheapside, a place of small shops, sheds and movable stalls for merchandise. Rykener was 'detected in women's clothing' while 'committing that detestable, unmentionable and ignominious vice' with a client called John Britby. Britby, 'thinking he was a woman', had approached him in Cheap and asked if he might 'as he would a woman . . . commit a libidinous act with her' whereupon Rykener asked for money. The nature of the act is not specified; it might be anything from fellatio to anal intercourse. They had been using one of the stalls when they were taken up.

In the course of his examination before the city officers Rykener revealed that he been taught his trade by Anna, 'the whore of a former servant of Sir Thomas Blount'. He had then learned how to dress as a woman in the household of an embroiderer, Elizabeth Brouderer, and that in Brouderer's house he had sexual intercourse with a priest 'as with a woman'. The priest, Philip, came from Theydon Garnon in Essex and may not have been used to urban wiliness. Rykener took two of the priest's gowns, no doubt as a form of payment, and, when asked to return them, he replied that he was 'the wife of a certain man and that, if Philip wished to ask for them back, he would make his husband bring suit upon him'. Rykener was a thief and blackmailer as well as prostitute, and casts an intriguing light on medieval London.

He then travelled up to Oxford, nominally as an embroiderer, where he and three scholars 'practiced the abominable vice often'. He was then employed as a tapster in the Swan Inn at Burford, where he had sex with two Franciscans, one Carmelite and six 'foreign men'. He confessed that on his return to London he had intercourse with three chaplains in the lanes behind St Katherine's by the Tower. In fact he had enjoyed intimacy with innumerable priests and friars, and really could not remember all their names. He confessed, too, that 'as a man' he enjoyed sexual intercourse with countless women, among them many nuns.

It is a queer story, with friars and nuns paying for different types of intercourse with the no doubt attractive and presumably effeminate youth. He was libidinous but was he homosexual, bisexual, heterosexual, or all of them at once? Once again the categories do not apply. Sexuality was a fluid, infinitely malleable and indefinite condition. It permeated the streets of London like the smell of pies and sweetmeats. The case ended inconclusively, and no further action seems to have been taken. Did the officials of the Guildhall simply not know how to proceed? Only the Church courts, in any case, could try offences of sodomy. But John Mirk's *Instructions to Parish Priests*, written in the late fourteenth century, advises other priests never to mention the subject to their congregations; they were not to teach or preach about it, for fear of corrupting the faithful. It was perhaps considered to be so attractive a sin that the very mention of it might provoke interest.

Rykener himself simply disappears. He may have made his way back to Foul Lane or Naked Boy Alley, to the kitchen gardens and latrines, the orchards and the cloisters. There was plenty of open space in the city. A raid by inspectors prompted the report that 'behind The Pie in Queenhithe is a privy place which is a good shadowing for thieves and many evil bargains have been made there'. Thomas Gresham's Royal Exchange soon became a place for queer assignations, and a male brothel was established opposite the Old Bailey. It was widely reported that barbers' shops, tailors and milliners were very good for custom, and were so thought in subsequent centuries. The young men who were employed in the fashionable clothes' shops of Ludgate Hill, in 1709, for example, were well known for effeminacy. *The Times* of 1857 called attention to 'the mincing and bowing' of drapers' assistants. It represents a long tradition.

Only one case of sodomy came before the Church courts of London in the fifteenth century. William Smyth announced publicly, no doubt from a street pulpit, that he had engaged in 'a sodomitic crime with master Thomas Tunley'. This sounds like a malicious attempt to compromise Tunley, and no further action was taken. In the same set of records Agnes Andrew testified that the husband of Margaret Myler was in fact a woman who was accustomed to 'grab' priests between their legs. Whether this was a case of male or female transvestism, or sheer calumny, is not clear; once more the case was set aside. Two further cases, of priests exposing their '*secreta sua*', or privy members, in public, complete the bare record.

We must travel much further for more news. In the Arap mosque of Istanbul two knights, Sir William Neville and Sir John Clanvowe, are buried side by side in a joint tomb. On their headstone are inscribed two helmets placed in such a position that they seem to be kissing, while their shields overlap. Both men were well acquainted with Chaucer and were no doubt part of the circle of 'Lollard knights' at the court of Richard II in London. They had travelled far to engage in a campaign by the Duke of Bourbon against Tunis. They would have been well rewarded, but for the fact that Clanvowe died during the campaign; the event, according to a monkish chronicle, provoked such 'inconsolable sorrow' in Neville 'that he never took food again and two days afterwards breathed his last, greatly mourned in the same village'. In a treatise on arms the herald gave the two knights the same arrangement of arms as a married couple, which confirms the natural supposition that they were in fact themselves married in some fashion. There are many examples of male friends being united in lasting bonds with oaths and ritual acts. We are once more at a loss in deciding what was really going on. The phrases used are 'sworn brothers' or 'wed brethren' in 'trouth-plight', and the term 'wedding' was applied both to two males as well as male and female. In a scrap of verse, written in the reign of Henry VI, come lines that tell the same story:

> Freris hase thame umbythoght, and sworne ilkane to other,
> Salle never no counte betyne mane bycomen ther brother.

The friars have sworn to one another that no cunt [woman] shall come between them.

The monks and friars of London were, however, soon to be sorely surprised. The hostility of Henry VIII against their faith, and his desire to exploit their riches, led him to attack what was considered their essential weakness. In 1533, two years before his officials 'visited' the monasteries in search of sin and wealth, the Buggery Act was passed. Buggery, or anal intercourse, was now deemed to be an offence worthy of death 'because there was not sufficient punishment for this abominable vice'. It became of pressing significance in this reign because of the official animus against the Roman Catholic establishment. In the reign of the monarch's father, Henry VII, queerness had not been a problem at all; Castiglione commented on the number of 'womanish men' at court.

Now all was changed. Catholicism was now 'the other', the shadowland, the source of treason, sin, crime and sickness. Those priests and friars who refused to assent to the Act of Supremacy in 1534, whereby Henry was proclaimed to be head of the Church in England, were rendered suspect. The Treasons Act, which shortly followed, declared such defiance as worthy of death by beheading or worse. Death was the fate of Thomas More and of John Fisher, and also of many other friars and monks. The Buggery Act, which gave Henry's officials licence to roam through the monasteries, convents and friaries in search of gold and other treasures, had led the way.

The Act proscribed same-sex activity within the circle of civil rather than ecclesiastical law. Buggery, a popular word that had replaced the biblical associations of sodomy, was unlawful as well as immoral; as so often with the king's commandments, a measure designed for specific purposes had wide and unintended consequences. The desire of the king for the wealth of the Church had turned a sin into a crime. The Buggery Act was repealed and then restored in the Tudor period. According to the members of Elizabeth's first parliament, as a result of the repeal under the Catholic Queen Mary Tudor, 'diverse evil disposed persons have been the more bold to commit the said most horrible and detestable vice of buggery aforesaid, to the high displeasure of almighty God'. Buggery had first been grouped with sorcery and witchcraft but at a later stage sodomy and black magic were treated as separate crimes. Buggery was no longer a purely religious heresy but had implications for the whole of the body politic.

The Buggery Act of 1533 survived the turmoil of centuries in its various interpretations. It was eventually replaced in 1828, but sodomy remained a capital offence until 1861. Buggery in fact remains as part of the Sexual Offences Act of 2003.

So a new and brutal reality had entered the consciousness of Londoners. You could die for deeds done in the dark. A rap on the knuckles was replaced by the tug of a rope. One of the first to go was Lord Hungerford. Although he was formerly an associate of Henry VIII and of Thomas Cromwell, he was made to suffer as an example. He was accused of buggery with his male servants and, after a formal trial, was beheaded upon Tower Hill on 28 July 1540. Accusations of state treason against him may have muddied the waters but sodomy or buggery, call it what you will, was itself a form of treason.

It was fortunate that very few were prosecuted for buggery and that, of all the penal statutes, it was the one least used. The common understanding may have been that it was directed against the Catholic clergy, and once they had all but disappeared, there was no further use for it.

The visitations of the monasteries by the cohorts of the

Crown, however, netted a great many more of those who were considered to be criminals. The reports of Cromwell's agents, the contents of which were often elicited by threats and punishments, were so scandalous that they provoked universal condemnation. Monks were sleeping with monks, monks were sleeping with boys, boys were sleeping with whomever. Hugh Latimer, Protestant Bishop of Worcester, wrote that 'when their enormities were first read in the Parliament House, they were so great and abominable that there was nothing but "*Down with them*!"' That was of course the purpose of the exercise, and down they went. In 175 entries, the commissioners refer to 180 monks who were 'sodomites'. In 1546 John Bale's *The Acts of the English Votaries* accused the whole body of the clergy as 'none other than sodomites and whoremongers all the pack'. They have 'burned in their own lusts one to another . . . man with man . . . monk with monk, nun with nun, friar with friar and priest with priest'. This was 'abominable sodometry'. Bale groped far back, to the occasion of Pope Gregory complimenting the English slave boys. 'See how curious these fathers were,' he wrote, 'in the well eyeing of their wares.'

In *The Anatomy of Melancholy* Robert Burton specifically mentioned the year of 1538 when officials inspected the cloisters and dormitories where they found 'gelded youths, debaucheries, catamites, boy-things, pederasts, sodomites (as it saith in Bale), Ganymedes etcetera'. He added that 'I do not speak, meanwhile, of those obscenities, the true scarcely nameable self-defilement of the monks, those masturbators'. Richard Morison, in *A Remedy for Sedition* (1536), described 'how young novices may stand instead of young wives. I have said enough. It stinks too sour to be stirred so much.'

It was taken for granted that the Jesuits, in particular, practised and condoned sodomy. Ephraim Pagitt, in his *Heresiography*

(1645), claimed that 'these are the most pernicious and dangerous sort of all others. These are not ignorant sots like the Anabaptists, and others, but educated and brought up in all manner of humane learning, and so more able to do mischief. These take upon to justify all the error and abominations of Antichrist: yes, their idolatries and sodomitical uncleanness they will defend and maintain.' Roman Catholics could conceal their uncleanness, also, in the solemn secret of the confessional when no voice could be divulged to another. It was said that some men made a confession of buggery to the priests who had actually taken part in it with them, thus providing a double seal of silence. The act of confession itself was reported to be the occasion of seduction, and from the 1560s in Europe arose the closed and divided confessional box. It was no longer needed in England, where after the Reformation the tribal rites of confession and expiation were treated with horror.

Secrecy was no deterrent in London. Suspicion and rumour swirled about the streets of a locality, and one of the common phrases of the courts mentions that sexual irregularities provoked 'the great offence of the neighbours'. It has always been so in the city where sex, of various kinds, was a hot topic. Same-sex activity does not in fact often appear in the judicial or administrative records but was known to be a problem threatening the peace of the city and the integrity of the family. In 1563 Casiodoro del Reina, who ministered to a Spanish Protestant refugee church in London, was forced to flee the city with his seventeen-year-old lover after being accused of sodomy. He may have been the victim of a whispering campaign among the Lutheran community.

From the sixteenth century derives that loose association between Catholicism and same-sex love that was still invoked in the early twentieth century, when for example, mobs of the East End threatened newly established Catholic churches. In Evelyn Waugh's *Brideshead Revisited* (1945), Cousin Jasper gives advice to Charles Ryder on Oxford University. 'Beware the Anglo-Catholics. They're all sodomites with unpleasant accents.' The wearing of beards in the sixteenth century was seen as a Protestant gesture, whereas the smooth-faced cleric was suspect. In another bout of alchemical combination, Catholicism and the theatre have also been aligned, with actors routinely suspected of secret sins. Like priests at the Mass, they dress up and flap their hands. Like priests, they play a part and are surrounded by boys.

GANYMED.

6

Bring on the dancing boys

Men dressed as raucous females, and boys dressed as demure young ladies, accompanied the greatest age of theatre in London's history, which we may date from the last decades of the sixteenth to the early decades of the seventeenth century. They were as familiar and predictable as the trumpets and the tabors. In the mummings and moralities of the previous period, the cross-dressing of actors raised serious doubts about their sexuality. Some theatrical haunts were already notorious. In the mid-fifteenth century one drunken cleric, Master Robert Colynson, had burst into a doubtful tavern in Southwark where, according to the Patent Rolls, he wrapped his arms around a boy of eleven 'and kissed him many times as if he had been a woman'. The marshal of the King's Bench berated him, not for attacking the boy, but for drinking so early in the morning.

London was a site of erotic theatre. The codpieces were padded so that the cods looked plumper; the pointed tips of men's shoes were stuffed with sawdust so that they stood more erect. There was an old belief that the larger the feet, the longer the penis. The hose was tight, for the sake of the legs, and the doublet was short. This was the perfect costume for what were sometimes known as 'the young Ganymedes' who had learned to parade their wares upon the stage. Stephen Gosson wrote, in the *School of Abuse* (1579), that these boys employ 'effeminate gesture, to ravish the sense; and wanton speech to whet desire to inordinate lust'; the theatres of the period 'effeminate the mind, as pricks unto vice'.

Filth was piled on filth when the boys dressed up as girls so that 'in that vice the putting of women's attire may kindle in men unclean affections'. When these transvestite boy actors 'do but touch men only with their mouth, they put them to wonderful pain and make them so mad: so beautiful boys by kissing do sting and pour secretly in a kind of poison, the poison of incontinence'. And the madness is this: the male lover does not see or care whether the object of his lust is male or female. His is an undifferentiated lust, raging and advancing, that poses one of the greatest threats to the commonwealth of citizens.

Two boy actors, playing Sly and Sinklo, are part of the introduction to John Marston's *The Malcontent* (1603).

> SLY: Oh cousin, come, you shall sit between my legs here.
> SINKLO: No, indeed, cousin: the audience will then take me for a viol-de-gamba, and think that you play upon me.
> SLY: Nay, rather that I work upon you, coz.

The great London playhouses, including the Theatre and the Curtain, were little better than pickup joints for queer men. The acting companies were, therefore, schools for scandal. In Ben Jonson's *Poetaster* (1601) Ovid learns that his son is to become an actor. 'What? Shall I have my son a stager now, an ingle for players?' Edward Guilpin, in *Skialetheia* (1598), describes a sodomite as one 'who is at every play and every night sups with his ingles'.

Some male members of the audiences came especially to watch a favourite boy, perhaps in a woman's part. The playwright Thomas Dekker invites the gallants in the audience to pay a little more in order to come upon the stage where 'you may (with small cost) purchase the dear acquaintance of the boys'.

The evidence suggests that there was a large conclave of queers who knew each other, if only by sight, and used the theatres as their meeting places. From the evidence of the plays themselves they shared jokes and puns and risky allusions. It might be going too far to suggest that they were a 'community', in any accepted sense of the word, but they were a strong and recognisable presence in the public spaces of London. Two of their favourite haunts, the theatres of Whitefriars and Blackfriars, specialised in boy actors or, as Middleton put it, 'a nest of boys able to ravish a man'. Whitefriars, in particular, specialised in homoerotic plays which dealt in vulgarities and obscenities; a dedicated audience no doubt enjoyed the pun and the fun. The humour itself was broad and bawdy. 'My office is italianated,' one character in *The Turke* explains, 'I am fain to come behind.' References abound to bums and pricks, erections and dildoes, inches and bits, amorous dew and quick flesh.

Whitefriars was run by playwrights, itself unusual, and was situated in a dubious area of London by the river; it was a 'private' or enclosed theatre. Two brothels nearby were known as 'Sodom' and 'Little Sodom'. Ram Alley, of dubious reputation, was a thoroughfare in Whitefriars. It is easy to understand how such a theatre could attract a group of devotees. Plays with titles such as *Ram Alley* and *Maids of Moreclacke* were very popular and contained such stock characters as the randy virgin and the fat whore. Vulgar innuendo has always been part of English comedy.

This was the essential reason why the Puritans detested modern drama. In *Histriomastix* (1632) William Prynne denounces 'modern examples of such, who have been desperately enamoured of players' boys thus clad in women's apparel so far as to solicit them by words, by letters, even actually to abuse them'. He also reaffirms the idea of 'secret conclaves'. But the Puritans' rage against effeminacy is evidence that relationships in the theatrical world between men and boys were conducted openly and were characteristically treated tolerantly or casually. The nature of dual desire was taken for granted.

Four years after the publication of the *School of Abuse* Philip Stubbes continued the attack on theatrical queerness in *The Anatomy of Abuses* (1583) by marking 'the flocking and running to theatres and curtains, daily and hourly, night and day, time and tide, to see plays and interludes, where such wanton gestures, such bawdy speeches: such laughing and fleering: such kissing and bussing: such clipping and culling: such winking and glancing of wanton eyes, and the like is used, as is wonderful to behold. Then these goodly pageants being done, every mate sorts to his mate, everyone brings another homeward of their way very friendly, and in their secret conclaves (covertly) they play the sodomites or worse.'

The 'secret conclaves' that so exercised Stubbes were not necessarily in the household where prying eyes and ears might be alert. Stubbes intimates that 'in the fields and suburbs of the city they have gardens, either paled or walled about very high, with their arbours and bowers fit for the purpose . . . And for that their gardens are locked, some of them have three or four keys a-piece, whereof one they keep for themselves, the other their paramours have to go in before them, lest haply they should be perceived, for then were all those sports dashed . . . these gardens are excellent places, and for the purpose; for if they can speak with their darlings nowhere else, yet they may be sure to meet them, and to receive the guerdon [reward] of their paines, they know best what I mean.' Yet gardens were not the only ports of call. Prynne also notes that these 'godless persons now swarm so thick of late in the streets of our Metropolis'.

Lord Hunsdon was suspected of keeping a male brothel at Hoxton, not a million miles from the Curtain and other suburban playhouses. 'Male stews' are mentioned in John Marston's *The Scourge of Villany* (1598). The writer creates the persona of Luscus who leaves his wife alone with a monkey and a porcelain dildo, a singularly unappetising scenario.

> At Hogsdon now his monstrous lusts he feasts,
> For there he keeps a bawdy house of beasts.

In another of his works, *The Metamorphosis of Pygmalion's Image* (1598), Marston (who betrays a close interest in such matters) describes a 'Ganymede' who 'for two days' space is closely hired' – is, in other words, secretly hired for sex. The young male prostitute was a person of interest to contemporaries. As Thomas Middleton put it in 1599:

> But truth to tell a man or woman whether,
> I cannot say she's excellent in either,
> But if report may certify a truth,
> She's neither or either, but a cheating youth.

An Italian/English dictionary, compiled by John Florio, has an example of '*Catamito*: one hired to sin against nature, an ingle, a Ganymede'. Pages in private households were sometimes hired for other than purely domestic purposes. A male prostitute was also known as a 'dog'.

Actors themselves were commonly suspected of sodomy. They were not 'real' men but posing as such. Some lines from Shakespeare's *Coriolanus* catch the mood:

> ... and I have nightly since
> Dreamt of encounters 'twixt thyself and me;
> We have been down together in my sleep,
> Unbuckling helms, fisting each other's throat,
> And waked half dead with nothing.

Homosexual passion also comes to the surface in *The Merchant of Venice*, *Twelfth Night*, *Othello* and in those plays where cross-dressing is of significance. It is a passion closely evinced by the author of the sonnets to his favoured boy. In Shakespeare's work, too, there are a host of words for the penis as well as insistent references to sodomy, buggery and fellatio. In *Love's Labour's Lost*, Armado declares that he allows his master 'with his royall finger thus' to 'dallie with my excrement'. This may be an expression of Shakespeare's interest in such matters, but it may simply have been a representation of the reality all around him.

With the possible exception of Christopher Marlowe, Shakespeare may legitimately be considered as the greatest of English homoerotic poets, thus tying together drama and buggery with threads of gold.

Christopher Marlowe himself had a reputation, if the phrase attributed to him that 'all they that love not tobacco and boys are fools' be true. Richard Baines, a double agent, accused him of stating that 'St John the Evangelist was bedfellow to Christ and leaned always in his bosom; that he used him as the sinners of Sodoma'. It is widely supposed that the pastoral lyric opening 'Come live with me and be my love' is addressed to one of the boys of London, although its ambiguity in the matter is part of its power. Marlowe was less coy in an early passage of his play *Edward II* (1593), about the king who fell in love with Piers Gaveston:

Sometimes a lovely boy in Dian's shape
With hair that gilds the water as it glides . . .
And in his sportful hands an olive tree,
To hide those parts which men delight to see.

Queer drama is complemented by queer poetry. In his first published poem, *The Affectionate Shepherd* (1594), Richard Barnfield declares:

If it be sin to love a lovely lad,
Oh then sin I.

In the same poem his thoughts are:

Of that fair boy that had my heart entangled
Cursing the time, the place, the sense, the sin:
I came, I saw, I viewed, I slipped in.

The last line is very crisp. It is at one with the allusions to back doors, back passages and postern gates that are frequently to be found in the verse of the period. The mysterious commentator of Edmund Spenser's *The Shepherd's Calendar*, known only as 'E.K.', notes of one passage that 'in this place seems to be some savour of disorderly love, which the learned call pederastic'. To which he adds 'and so is pederastic much to be preferred before gynerastic, that is the love which enflames men with lust towards womankind'.

In the context of Elizabethan London, queerness was no great sin. Young men at the inns of court, and the turbulent ranks of the apprentices, were merely the most rowdy members of a male culture that excluded any female presence and was therefore susceptible to what one contemporary described as 'filthy and detestable loves, horrible lusts, incest and buggery'. Even the schoolboys who parsed and construed their Latin were exposed to sodomitical allusions in the pastoral poetry of Virgil and the elegies of Ovid. So in the 'argument' of Virgil's *Bucolics*, translated in 1575, they would have found 'Corydon, a shepherd unreasonably in love with a passing fair youth named Alexis, and seeking him up and down in wayless woods and places void of passage, rehearses all things which might or could obtain love and liking'. Such interpolations were part of the masculine culture that dominated school and university. It was literally beaten into the boys. 'My master has beat me so,' one boy wrote, 'naked in his chamber.' It was a simple question of power. Sex with a younger male was the instrument or expression of that fact.

The relationships between masters and pupils were always suspect. Nicholas Udall, headmaster of Eton from 1534 to 1541, was called to London to be questioned on the rumours of scarlet sins. He was well known for inflicting severe corporal punishment on his boys and did indeed 'confess that he did commit buggery' several times with one of his pupils, Thomas Cheyne, who was accused of stealing silver. He had had sex with the boy on 'the sixth day of this present month in the present year [March 1541] at London'. He spent a brief period in the Marshalsea prison, before eventually being appointed as headmaster of the school at Westminster in the reign of Mary. He is perhaps best known for his work with boy actors and for the composition of one of the first comedies in English, *Ralph Roister Doister*, in which a boy plays a rich widow under siege from suitors.

The love for boys was often deemed to be sexually and morally superior to the love for women. It might be youthful infatuation among contemporaries, it might be Platonic idealism encouraged by a Renaissance humanist education, or it might just be lust. It could of course be a blancmange of all three. Many reasons were given at the time, pre-eminently in the English translations of Greek and Latin fables where the love of boys was prominent. The boys were prettier than women. They did not wear perfume or make-up. They were more natural and more artless in lovemaking; they did not make such a fuss about it. There were fewer unfortunate consequences in the nursery way.

And in any case there were other possibilities. As Sir Voluptuous Beast in Jonson's epigram explained to his new wife: 'And how his Ganymede mov'd, and how his goat'. This is supplemented by Donne's account of the court in the 1590s where is it is not difficult to discover 'who loves whores, who boys and who goats'. The goat may be more of a satirical topos, however, than a reality.

By certain signs you may know them. Many physiognomical treatises, published in the sixteenth century, are very clear about the characteristics of the queer. His eyebrows are very straight, demonstrating weakness and femininity; small nostrils are the signs of a small penis, and if his nose is turned upwards a little you may suspect him. His chin is round rather than, as it should be, square; his knees are loose and turn outwards; so do his hips. If he has a mole on his ankle, he will take the passive part. He breathes deeply and rapidly. He trembles. His face and eyes move at the same time. If he is to be cured of his deplorable condition he must reside in a hot and windy place, and eat hot rustic foods.

Notorious cases made for profitable reading. In 1580 Edward de Vere, Earl of Oxford, accused two Elizabethan courtiers, Francis Southwell and Henry Howard, of treasonable activities.

They in turn accused Oxford of sodomy 'by buggering a boy that is his cook and many other boys'. He was alleged to have said that 'when women were unsweet, fine (young) boys were in season'. You could turn your hand to one or the other according to the weather or the time of day. It was not a question of either/or but of both. It was performing an act, not affirming an identity.

Sodomy, therefore, was known to be part of the human condition, which is not to say that it was well understood. It was sometimes blamed on drunkenness. It could be laughed off. It could be overlooked or dismissed as tittle-tattle. One minister, accused of the act, said that he had committed it in his sleep. Even as he did it, he may not have known what he was doing. The bewilderment might have been equally genuine among many other people. They could not conceive of themselves as 'sodomites', a charge equivalent to treason or heresy. They were just doing what had always been done. It could be that same-sex activity often went unrecognised and undeclared, or was simply ignored.

GEORGE VILLIERS Duke of BUCKINGHAM &c.

7

Soft and slippery

By the first years of the seventeenth century homoeroticism had become a distinct flavour both in public and in private life. It had come to the point that, according to the notebook of an early-seventeenth-century official, Sir Thomas Wilson, 'some men will be apt to think that any man uses it [sodomy] that has but a young boy or man to serve him, or that he uses his servants in his chamber'. So once more it was a question of power. In 1609 a London merchant, Richard Finch, was charged with the abuse of his servant and of 'correcting him unreasonably with whipcords, being quite naked'. It is not clear whether master or servant was naked, but common sense suggests the latter. It was believed that sodomy was everywhere. There seems to have been little need for reticence or concealment; a queer language, with pointed allusions, became the mode; vulgarity and obscenity were commonplace, and nowhere more so than at the newly established court of James I.

The king enjoyed the presence of male companions and, according to reports stronger than rumour, favoured certain male lovers. A disapproving witness, Lucy Hutchinson, stated that the court had been full of 'fools and bawds, mimics and catamites'. It might have been the court of William Rufus strangely revived. The king's hunting lodge at Royston was staffed entirely by men. He liked them smooth-faced and young. He cuddled them and 'pressed' them; sometimes he literally drooled over them. He was in many respects uncouth, and was observed to fiddle with his codpiece.

One of the first of James's favourites was Robert Carr, created Earl of Somerset, to whom the king once complained of 'your long creeping back and withdrawing yourself from lying in my chamber, notwithstanding my many hundred times earnestly soliciting you to the contrary'.

His last and greatest favourite was George Villiers, 1st Duke of Buckingham, who signed himself to the king as 'Your Majesty's humble slave and dog'. 'Dog' could, as we have seen, be used as a slang word for catamite. In one letter, Buckingham asked the king whether he loved him as much as the time 'at Farnham, where the bed's head could not be found between the master and his dog'. It is a tricky allusion, to be deciphered as you will. Some of this may indeed have been a great game, a sport of wild and wilder innuendo, with no realistic basis. Buckingham once referred to James's 'large bountiful hand', for example, and went on to explain that 'there is this difference between that noble hand and heart, one may surfeit by the one, but not by the other, and sooner by yours than his own'. This may suggest in an indirect way that their pleasures went no further than mutual masturbation, thus skirting the shores of sodomy.

Other letters are not so sportive. In the months before his death the king wrote, in his own hand, a remarkably intimate missive to Buckingham in which he pledged to make with him 'a new marriage, ever to be kept hereafter, for, god so love me, as I desire only to live in this world, for your sake, & that I had rather live banished in any part of the world with you, than live a sorrowful widow's life without you, & so god bless you my sweet child & wife & grant that you may ever be a comfort to your dear dad and husband'. Scholars have argued over the purport of the letter, with some suggesting that it is part of the rite of 'sworn brothers' with no sexual content. Others, noting 'wife' and 'widow' and 'husband', have suggested something more. The king himself seems to have been defiant. 'Jesus Christ did the same,' he is reported as saying, 'and therefore I cannot be blamed. Christ had his John, and I have my George.' He was overheard when he visited Buckingham lying sick from a toothache. 'Begott man never loved another more than I do you and let God leave me when I leave you.'

The debate about the exact nature of their relationship is now of little moment. It can confidently be stated, however, that the letter from king to duke is a queer letter indeed. It is queer because it is unfastened from sexual and social categories and has drifted into some formless space where innuendo and meaning can multiply. This is the context in which it was observed that the women at the court of James I adopted more masculine clothing, and that the male courtiers were more effeminately dressed than in the previous reign. A contemporary observer and memoirist, Francis Osborne, noted that the king's affection for his favourites 'was as amorously conveyed as if he had mistaken their sex, and thought them ladies; which I have seen Somerset and Buckingham labour to resemble, in the effeminateness of their dressings'. Osborne added that the king's love, 'or what else posterity will please to call it', was not 'carried on with a discretion sufficient to cover a less scandalous behaviour; for the king's kissing them after so lascivious mode in public, and upon the theatre, as it were, of the world prompted many to imagine some things done in the tyring house [where the actors changed their dress]'. A mock-tribute to the king, *Corona Regia* (1615), so enraged James that he instituted a hunt for the author and publisher;

their crime had been to detail the succession of young men whom he had once favoured under the guise of 'advancing the beautiful'.

An anonymous tract complained that 'he must have the public to be witness of his lascivious tongue licking of his favourites' lips . . . and his hands must be seen in a continual lascivious action'. It is fairly clear, therefore, that his homoeroticism was on open display. John Oglander, knighted by the king, remarked that 'I never saw any fond husband make so much or so great dalliance over his beautiful spouse as I have seen King James over his favourites, especially the Duke of Buckingham'.

This was indeed a complaisant court. Another observer, Sir Simonds D'Ewes, noted that the 'boys were grown to the height of wickedness to paint'. He recorded in 1622 that he discussed with a friend matters that 'were secret as of the sin of sodomy, how frequent it was in this wicked city'. He followed this observation with a story of an usher in a school, a Frenchman, who had buggered a knight's son and was brought into the Guildhall 'and had surely received his just punishment, but that [Sir Henry] Montague then chief justice was sent to save him, and by the king, as it was thought'. Why should the king wish to save an obscure French teacher from the charge of buggery?

Sir Francis Bacon, Lord Chancellor of England by 1618, is another queer case at court. A historian in 1653, Arthur Wilson, noted that Bacon's favours to his 'young, prodigal, and expensive' servants 'opened a gap to infamous reports'. They were a tribe of Ganymedes and he was their Zeus. In his *Brief Lives* John Aubrey reports that Bacon was 'a paiderastes'; his favourites took bribes but he himself was notably impartial in his judicial dealings. His own mother had her doubts, which she expressed to another of her sons, Anthony. 'I pity your brother,' she wrote in 1593, when Bacon was thirty-two, 'yet he pities not himself but keeps that bloody Percy . . . as a coach companion and bed companion – a proud profane and costly fellow, whose being about him I truly feel the Lord God does mislike and does the less bless your brother in credit and otherwise in his health.' Anthony Bacon himself was also suspected of sodomy with his servants but once again the case was never pressed against him.

In 1603 Bacon had written a philosophic and educational treatise entitled *The Masculine Birth of Time*, at the end of which he implores an unknown reader 'my dear, dear boy . . . from my inmost heart, give yourself to me so that I may restore you to yourself' and 'secure an increase beyond all the hopes and prayers of ordinary marriages'. 'Masculine love', the preliminary to 'masculine birth', was well-known shorthand for same-sex intimacy. In 1619 a sermon was preached against Bacon's 'catamites'.

The accusation or suspicion of sodomy did not lead to his expulsion from the court, but in 1621 charges of bribery and malfeasance proved to be his ruin. He spent two or three days in the Tower before being released, but he never enjoyed public service again. Simonds D'Ewes reported that, despite his disgrace, Bacon

> would not relinquish the practice of his most horrible and secret sin of sodomy, keeping still one Godrick, a very effeminate faced youth, to be his catamite and bedfellow, although he had discharged the most of his other household servants: which was the more to be admired [wondered at] because men after his fall began to discourse of that his unnatural crime which he had practiced for many years . . . which caused some bold and forward man to write these verse in a whole sheet of paper,

and to cast it down in some part of York House in the Strand, where Viscount St Alban [Bacon] yet lay:

> 'Within this sty a hog does lie
> That must be hanged for sodomy.'

So his inclinations were widely known in the city. The hog that sizzles becomes bacon. In his diary Bacon records his methodical use of enemas to cool his blood.

The records of the Middlesex Sessions testify to the fact that there were more cases of sodomy in London than anywhere else in the kingdom, even though it was still exceptional. It was difficult to prove that 'carnal knowledge' had ever taken place if the two parties were consenting; they could not testify against one another without implicating themselves. There also had to be two witnesses for the offence. Any accused was granted trial by jury, and could refuse to testify. Emission without penetration was no crime; that is why male intimacy sometimes only took place between the thighs. There may have been blows, and beatings, and bullying in the streets, for those suspected of sodomy; but nothing happened in the courts. It was not considered to be sufficiently dangerous. In any case the judges seem to have been more interested in disorder between men and women.

Some allusions of the period, however, are entirely specific. It was widely reported that the Duke of Buckingham had married off one of his female relations to Sir Anthony Ashley 'who never loved any but boys'. Alban Cooke, from the parish of Hoxton, was indicted for buggery with a male below the age of twenty; he was acquitted. Richard Walker of Castle Baynard was arrested for 'abusing himself in an ale-house'.

Edward Bawde was accused of buggery, but it was determined that it was a malicious prosecution by those who wanted to blackmail or to injure him. A Puritan tradesman, Nehemiah Wallington, reported he had just heard of a group of married men in Southwark 'who had "lived in the sin of buggery and were sworn brothers to it" some seven years, committing this sin on Sabbath mornings "at sermon time"'.

An informer, William Reynolds, denounced one Captain Edmonds for unnatural acts. 'He dwells in London. He was corporal general of the horse in Ireland under the Earl of Southampton. He ate and drank at his table and lay in his tent. The Earl of Southampton gave him a horse which Edmonds refused a hundred marks for him. The Earl of Southampton would coll [embrace] and hug in his arms and play wantonly with him.'

One sexual practice was often mentioned indirectly. Thomas Nashe agrees that if he is proved to be a rhymer and a railer 'he will give his tongue to wipe [his opponent's] tail with'. Another hack of the period, Anthony Nixon, describes his enemy as one 'who wipes vice's tail with his tongue, and that is the reason why his words are so unsavoury'. A flatterer is described by Richard Nicholls as 'he whose tongue the tail of greatness licks'.

The violent rape of a boy under age was the most heinous of offences and, if proven, incurred death. Sir Edward Coke, the jurist, noted that 'Humphrey Stafford, a known paederastes, on 12 May 1606 in the parish of Saint Andrew, High Holborn, led astray by the instigation of the devil, did with force and with arms assault a certain K.B. a lad of about sixteen years of age and at that time he did wickedly and in a manner diabolical, felonious and contrary to nature, have sexual relations with K.B. and at the same time had sex with R and did perpetrate with R that abominable and detestable sin of sodomy'. Coke noticed, too, that sodomy derived from pride, excess of diet, idleness and contempt for the poor.

A contemporary pamphlet alleged that Stafford had raped both boys at once. He had been so violent that the parents claimed 'they were forced to use the help of a surgeon for their care'. For his part Stafford pleaded only to drunkenness and said that 'if he had offended, it was in wine'; he also confessed that 'I acknowledge that I have deserved death, but yet I could not perform mine intention'. Nevertheless he was tried and sentenced to death; his execution in 1608 entertained 'a great throng and mass of people'.

So at court the act was covered or concealed by the use of allusion or euphemism; in public, in the streets of London, it was still punishable by death. Two lines from Jonson's *Epicoene* (1609) may complete the picture.

> BOY: I am the welcomest thing under a man that comes there.
>
> CLERIMONT: I think, and above a man too, if the truth were racked out of you.

Jonson, Marston and others single out sodomy for the particular objects of their attack. This unease about sexual roles, in the early part of the seventeenth century, was perhaps generated by the possibility that the king was a sodomite.

The 'womanish men', taking their cue from the court of the king, were also on display. They were 'womanly', they were 'childish'; they were 'delicate' and 'nice'. They were 'sweet smelling', 'comely arrayed', 'wantonly dressed up' and 'smug'. They were 'soft', 'pliant' and 'loose' but were also 'fearful, unconstant, wavering' and 'slippery'. This is perhaps the setting in which James I 'the peacemaker' may most profitably be found. He was well known for an aversion to weapons flourished in his presence, not at all an unreasonable attitude after his violent and threatened adolescence. He was also opposed to war, and was sometimes criticised for his pacific nature. His son, soon to become Charles I, tried to bully him into war with Spain. But his final hours came too soon. It is reported that he died holding the head of Buckingham. He remained soft and slippery to the end.

The Roaring Girle.

OR

Moll Cut-Purſe.

As it hath lately beene Acted on the Fortune-ſtage by *the Prince his Players.*

Written by *T. Middleton* and *T. Dekkar.*

Printed at *London* for *Thomas Archer*, and are to be ſold at his ſhop in Popes head-pallace, neere the Royall Exchange. 1611.

8

The rubsters

The story of same-sex love among women was bequeathed another chapter with the rediscovery of the clitoris by anatomists of the mid sixteenth century. It had been known to the Greeks but then disappeared from view. It could not have come as a surprise to women themselves that some organ or other was capable of arousal, but finally it had been named. A medical compendium of 1615, Helkiah Crooke's *Microcosmographia*, announced that the clitoris 'comes of an obscene word signifying contrectation [touching or fingering] but properly it is called the woman's yard [penis]. It is a small production in the upper, forward . . . and middle fatty part of the share [genitals] in the top greater cleft where the Nymphs [labia] do meet and is answerable to the member of the man.' The member of the man need have nothing to do with it, however, and the reintroduction of the clitoris heralded the rise in public awareness of the tribade, the fricatrix, the rubster. These were the women who knew how to manipulate 'the seat of women's delight' with a hand, a dildo or a massively enlarged clitoris.

Helkiah Crooke himself remarked that 'sometimes it grows to such a length that it hangs without the cleft like a man's member, especially when it is fretted with the touch of the clothes, and so struts and grows to a rigidity as does the yard of a man. And this part it is which those wicked women do abuse called Tribades (often mentioned by many authors, and in some states worthily punished) to their mutual and unnatural lusts.' It is sometimes suggested that lesbianism was, before the twentieth century, an unmentioned and invisible act; in fact it has a historical identity arguably as long as that of love between men. Wherever there are bodies, there are lovers. It is found, for example, at the end of the twelfth century, in a vision of Edmund, a monk of Eynsham Abbey. He was taken to purgatory and led to that site where the souls of those guilty of same-sex love were consigned for their own particular suffering. To his astonishment, among them were a great number of women. He was surprised because he had not suspected women to be capable of such a deed. But there they were, suspended in woe and pain.

A more mundane account, contained in William Harrison's *Description of England*, published in the latter part of the sixteenth century, alludes to the fact that certain women 'wore doublets with pendant codpieces on the breast', which was by any standard a queer form of dress, and that he had 'met with some of those trulls in London so disguised that it has passed my skill to discern whether they were men or women'. He adds that 'while they are in condition women, and would seem in apparel men, they are neither men nor women but plain monsters'. In his *Anatomy of Melancholy* (1621) Robert Burton also alludes to 'those wanton-loined womanlings, Tribadas, that fret each other by turns'. Some references are more vague or tentative. Thomas Harman in his *Caveat or Warning for Common Cursitors* (1566) remarks on a barn of beggars where every man had a woman, 'except it were two women that lay alone together for some especial cause'. This is the context that prompted Lady Anne Clifford to confess that 'my cousin Frances got the key of my chamber and lay with me which was the first time I loved her so very well'.

Same-sex love between women had been recognised for

many centuries before that, of course, and in his epistle to the Romans Paul referred to the vile behaviour of pagans when their women 'did change that natural use into that which is against nature'. St Ambrose amplified the picture by stating that 'it came about that a woman would desire a woman for the use of foul lust'. The fact that Queen Victoria seems never to have heard of it is unusual. It has always been here.

One of the most famous 'roaring girls' of London was Long Meg who kept a seedy tavern in Islington and generally dressed as a man to brave all newcomers who came to laugh at her or challenge her. A Frenchman accosted her but 'Meg met him and without any salute, fell to blows; after a long combat, she overcame him, and cut off his head. Then pulling off her hat, her hair fell about her ears.' In a popular penny pamphlet, *The Life and Pranks of Long Meg of Westminster* (1590), it is written that 'it chanced one evening that Meg in a frolic humour did put on a suit of man's apparel, and with her sword and buckler walked the streets'. A young nobleman approached her and made fun of her to which she replied with 'a good box on the ear'. It is not clear whether she was a 'real' person, however, and she may have been largely shaped through the medium of folklore and city legend. Invented or imagined characters sometimes walk the streets among the people. But Long Meg does at least represent an identifiable urban type of the sixteenth century.

She was not alone. One contemporary observer, in a pamphlet curiously entitled *Hic Mulier: or The Man-Woman: Being a Medicine to Cure the Coltish Disease of the Staggers in the Masculine-Feminine of Our Times* (1620), complained that the women of the day had divested themselves of the hood and the dress in order to sport broad-brimmed hats, pointed doublets and 'ruffianly short locks'. They desired to be 'man-like not only from the head to the waist, but to the very foot, and in every condition . . . and in brief so much man in all things, that they are neither men nor women, but just good for nothing'. They were often considered to be prostitutes: to be 'man-like' suggested that they had become sexually promiscuous and so, paradoxically, the woman who dressed as a man might be looking for other men. Contemporaries were confused. In the same year a companion volume was published. *Haec Vir* assaulted men who assumed the characteristics of women with 'such softness, dullness and effeminate niceness that it would make Heraclitus himself laugh against his nature to see how palingly you languish in this weak entertained sin of womanish softness'. 'Gender bending', generally considered to be a feature of the late twentieth century, has a long history.

For a few years, approximately between 1620 and 1625, female transvestism in fact became a London fashion and the 'masculine feminine' was a recognisable persona on the stages of the theatres and in the streets of the city. James himself instructed the clergy of London 'to inveigh vehemently and bitterly in their sermons against the insolency of our women . . . some of them [wearing] stilettoes or poniards'.

The Puritan pamphleteer, Philip Stubbes, argued that 'our apparel was given as a sign distinctive to discern between sex and sex and therefore one to wear the apparel of another is to participate with the same and to adulterate the verity of her own kind. Wherefore these women may not improperly be called hermaphrodites, that is monsters of both kinds, half women, half men.'

We may assume that these 'masculine women' associated one with another and, in the custom of London, informal networks between them were established. Slowly there grew up among them a world of reference, perused all the more eagerly because it was almost non-existent before the sixteenth century. Medical anatomies and medical treatises, the travel writings of those who had ventured among the Eastern women, the plethora of semi-pornographic paintings of females in romantic or amorous mood, the veiled allusions to the subject in moral treatises and the jeering references in less elevated publications augmented the gossip and scandal of the day to provide a relatively well-informed understanding of queer women.

Other spirited women dressed *en travesti* and took on all the characteristics of a somewhat boisterous male. One such was Mary Frith, alias Moll Cutpurse, who seems to have earned her living as a fortune-teller and pimp. Her biography, *The Life of Mrs Mary Frith* (published in 1662, three years after her death), reveals that as a child 'a very tomrig or rumpscuttle she was, and delighted and sported only in boys' play and pastime, not minding or companying with the girls; many a bang or blow this hoiting procured her, but she was not so to be tamed or taken off from her rude inclinations . . . her needle, bodkin and thimble she could not think on quietly, wishing them changed into sword and dagger for a bout of cudgels'. The biography may be of dubious provenance, but it does reveal the temper of the time.

The Roaring Girl (1610) by Thomas Middleton and Thomas Dekker was a semi-fictional account of her well-known cross-dressed adventures. Unlike Long Meg, she had an authentic pedigree. She was born in the Barbican, in about 1584, and died in Fleet Street in 1659, becoming a thief, cutpurse and fence along the way. In the frontispiece to the play she is wearing doublet and breeches, brandishing a sword, wearing a high 'copt' hat, and smoking a long pipe. In the summer of 1600 she was indicted at Middlesex Sessions for stealing two shillings and eleven pence.

She appeared as herself on the stage of the Fortune Theatre, according to a contemporary account, 'in man's apparel and in her boots and with a sword by her side, she told the company there present that she thought many of them were of opinion that she was a man but if any of them would come to her lodging they should find that she was a woman and some other immodest and lascivious speeches she also used at the time'. At the end of her performance she played upon a lute and sang. It is a fair bet that her lyrics were thoroughly obscene.

Once, as a result of a wager, she rode from Charing Cross to Shoreditch dressed as a man; she waved a flag and blew on a trumpet at the same time. As a result of her queer ways she was sentenced to stand and do penance, wearing a white sheet, at St Paul's Cross; but this appeared to have little or no effect upon her irregular behaviour. A contemporary diarist, John Chamberlain, recorded that 'she wept bitterly and seemed very penitent, but it is since doubted she was maudlin drunk, being discovered to have tippled of three quarts of sack before she came to her penance'. She had three mastiff dogs, each of which had its own bed with sheets and pillows. She was incarcerated in Bethlem Hospital for the insane, but was discharged. She dropped dead from the dropsy in the summer of 1659 and in her will stated that she wished to be buried 'with her breech upwards, that she might be as preposterous in her death as she had been all along in her infamous life'.

She is supposed to have disowned all interest in sexuality of any kind which might therefore mark her out as an asexual being. It would hardly be realistic to consider her as the prototype for a queer woman; this would be to confuse categories that did not then exist. She was not considered threatening, as a man in woman's dress might be, but something of a folly, an antic, a sport. She was in one sense paying homage to the

Elizabethan male by aping his manners and characteristics. She poured scorn on 'a contemporary as remarkable as myself, called Aniseed-water Robin, who was clothed very near my antic mode, being an hermaphrodite, a person of both sexes, him I could by no means endure'. She hired London boys to throw dirt at him. She was adduced as an example, in Havelock Ellis's *Studies in the Psychology of Sex* (six volumes, 1897–1928), of what he called 'the homosexual diathesis'. She could just as easily be called, in the language of the later twentieth century, a fetishistic transvestite, a lesbian, a latent transsexual or a hermaphrodite. She was just altogether queer; and there is something luscious and lusty about her queerness which suits the ripeness of the period. As a character in *The Roaring Girl* puts it, 'she slips from one company to another like a fat eel between a Dutchman's fingers'.

A strong or critical female mind was considered to be intrinsic to a masculine woman. When Ben Jonson was criticised by Cecelia Bulstrode, a member of the circle of women who assembled around the Countess of Bedford, he replied that 'What though with Tribade lust she force a Muse, / And in an Epicoene fury can write news . . .' 'Epicoene' in this context means 'of either gender', and in his play of the same name Jonson refers to a group of 'hermaphroditical collegiates'. The metaphors for a woman's love of the same sex were already deeply ingrained. This is the context for Thomas Nashe's *The Choice of Valentines* (1592), in which the dildo is the chosen object of desire: 'My little dildo shall supply their kind'.

Dildoes were known as 'shuttlecocks', and it was said that wanton or wicked men also liked to play the game with each other. The women seemed to like them even more, and the dildo was an indispensable element of queer play. A finger was often substituted. 'Take away your hand, I beseech you, from that place,' Agnes asks Angelica in *Venus in the Cloister* (1683), 'if you would not blow up a fire not easily to be extinguished.' In the same book is revealed 'a certain instrument of glass . . . she told him there were above fifty of them in their House [nunnery] and that everyone, from the abbess down to the last professed, handled them oftener than their beads'. 'I'm spilling' was the eighteenth-century equivalent of 'I'm coming'. In a play of 1640, Richard Brome's *The Antipodes*, Martha Joyless recalls one occasion when 'A wanton maid once lay with me, and kiss'd / And clipt, and clapt me strangely . . .'

Yet in the seventeenth century more dignified monuments may be found in the stillness of the grave. Anne Chitting and Mary Barber lay in the same tomb, in 1606, at the church of St James in Bury, Suffolk. The monument of 1710 to Mary Kendall and Lady Catharine Jones was established in the chapel of St John the Baptist in Westminster so that 'even their ashes, after death, might not be divided'. Catherine Jennings and Anne Fleming found their final sleep together at the vault of Wiveton parish church in Norfolk. Are we to deduce that these women were more than familiar companions? Nothing can be inferred, let alone proven, but they might perhaps have been silent witnesses for a condition which they did not disclose.

Queer sex among women was always a subject for pornography. Certain scenes in certain plays were designed to titillate what was probably a largely male audience; in the seventeenth century they were often translated from the Italian to be sold in London bookshops.

So what accounts for the silence of the women themselves? It is part of a larger silence. There is little knowledge of the personal lives of most females in most centuries. Women were of little significance and of even less interest. Their physical needs were considered to be concerned only with conception and parturition. It was of course known and understood that they could derive pleasure from sexual intercourse, but their desires were thought to be dangerous and therefore unmentionable. This was one of the reasons why queer sex between women was rarely mentioned; it might give certain women ideas. Since they were considered to be ruled by their bodies and by their passions, in some to the level of insatiability, there was no point in giving fresh occasion for sexual experiment. Women were known to be as frail as water. The crimes of men with men were proclaimed in courts of justice; the crimes of women with women were left unsaid. One observer stated that 'it is better that a woman give herself over to a libidinous desire to do as a man, than that a man make himself effeminate'.

The love of woman for woman was veiled behind the acceptance of close friendships between women; the general communication of warmth and affection was considered to be normal, and many queer women were able to mask their more fervent desires. For single women to live together was accepted and acceptable in every period. Women kissing and embracing was no occasion for comment.

If queer women did not challenge the conventional social order, they easily accommodated themselves to its rules. Only in the unlikely event that they threatened the reproductive cycle of marriage would they ever be punished.

Sex between women was not to be treated with any seriousness. There was no legal definition of lesbianism in any case because under English law no such condition existed. A woman could not penetrate another woman. It was a non-event, a nothing. A woman was a passive receptacle and nothing more. Love without a penis was not love at all. The uterus was considered to be an inverted penis, having therefore lost its primary function. It was believed that men and woman shared the same characteristics, except that the various bits were in different places. As *Aristotle's Masterpiece* (1684) puts it:

> For those that have the strictest searchers been
> Find woman are but men turned outside in;
> And men, if they but cast their eyes about,
> May find they're women with their inside out.

By the late seventeenth century, however, some women writers were beginning to touch upon the subject of same-sex love. In that period Aphra Behn and the Duchess of Newcastle deal with the sensitive topic in a predominantly chaste, reserved or romantic fashion, but it is nonetheless there. The duchess, for example, imagines two female characters kissing 'with more alacrity than women use, a kind of titillation'. In her collection of poems *Lycidus: or the Lover in Fashion* (1688), Behn addresses an indeterminate figure who might be male or female:

> In pity to our Sex sure thou wer't sent
> That we might Love, and be innocent:
> For sure no Crime with thee we can commit.

Behn herself had already entered the masculine world as a spy in Antwerp for Charles II, but her fame rested on stories, poems and nineteen plays. She was prolific and was often accused of adopting a 'masculine' and bawdy style. In her play *The False Count* (1681), one character touches upon lesbianism in a thoroughly contemporary way: 'I have known as much danger hidden under a Petticoat, as a pair of Breeches. I have heard of two Women that married each other – oh abominable . . .'

Margaret, Duchess of Newcastle, otherwise known as 'Mad

Madge', began her literary career just below the age of thirty in 1652 in the quest 'to make ourselves as free, happy and famous as men'. In her subsequent writings she encroached upon what were considered to be male preserves in science and philosophy, atomic theory and political satire, epistemology and chemical experiment; her favourite among her twenty-three volumes was *Philosophical and Physical Opinions* (1655). She was also a devotee of what she called 'singularity' of dress and demeanour and as a result became the talk of the town. When she designed her own dress which revealed 'scarlet trimmed nipples' or when she appeared festooned with lace ribbons, crowds gathered to gape at her.

Katherine Phillips, also known as 'the Matchless Orinda', addressed passionate but not pornographic poems to women. In a letter to a female friend she writes of 'my vast desires to enjoy you'. And in her poetry she describes 'spotless passion' which will never 'spend our stock by use'.

The male impersonators of the women are, as usual, much more vulgar. John Donne wrote in the persona of Sappho; he and his fellow poet, Thomas Woodward, imagined their mutual inspiration to be a queer love in a 'mystical tribadry' in which Woodward's Muse 'rubbed and tickled' that of Donne 'to spend some of her pith'. Female sexuality, as it gradually became visible in the higher circles of poets and wits, was likely to be the subject of coarse male jokes compounded of fantasy and lust. A poem of 1673, by Edward Howard, refers to 'Two females meeting, found a sportful way / Without man's help a tickling game to play'.

On 12 September 1680, James Howard and Arabella Hunt walked down the aisle of Marylebone Church in order to be united in marriage. For the next six months, according to a witness, they lived together 'as man and wife at bed and board'. Yet James Howard was a female, otherwise known as Mrs Amy Poulter, who had been married to a Mr Poulter for eight years. Her husband was still alive when Amy became a husband herself. When the odd couple came to light Amy defended her marriage to Arabella Hunt as arranged 'not seriously but rashly and unduly and in a frolic jocular or facetious manner'. This was queer enough, but it was also testified that Amy had in fact dressed as a female in order to court Arabella. The fact that they had also shared a bed for six months suggests that both women did indeed know the true sex of 'James Howard' and were inclined to keep it a secret. Mrs Hunt, Arabella's mother, seems to have colluded in the subterfuge by arranging for the marriage to take place in a church out of the way. The motives for family and friends cannot now be understood, but it has been suggested that the Hunts hoped to benefit from a union, however exotic, with the more affluent Poulters.

Four years later, in 1684, a pamphlet was issued with the title of *The She-Wedding: or a mad Marriage, between Mary, a Seaman's Mistress, and Margaret, a Carpenter's Wife, at Deptford*. Mary was pregnant, but her lover was on the high seas. How could she persuade the sailor's family to support her and her infant? Her friend, Margaret, came to her rescue. Margaret disguised and dressed herself as man before going through a marriage ceremony with Mary. The marriage was then entered in the parish register where it was antedated by a corrupt parson. They lived as man and wife for six weeks before being discovered, whereupon they were incarcerated. Two or three cases may not amount to much but they do lead to speculation that other such clandestine marriages between women have gone unrecorded.

Some women were undoubtedly masculine by instinct, as

has been seen, and not by sexual orientation. They might dress up as sailors and soldiers, brave the vicissitudes of the sea and charge the enemy. As a result they were generally admired. They had surpassed their sex, and any hint of queerness was dissipated by their usual return to a husband and domesticity. Some of them opened public houses on the merits of their reputation; others took to the stage or the circus. Marianne Rebecca Johnson worked aboard a collier, the *Mayflower*, without once being suspected; she had consigned herself to service in fear of an abusive stepfather. Anne Chamberlayne, 'fought under her brother', according to her memorial stone, 'with arms and manly attire, in a fire-ship, for six hours on 20 June 1690'. The cross-dressing women were not often the target of obloquy or mockery. They were praised for their hardiness and for their ambition. They were attempting to be 'as good as' men.

When in 1693 Ralph Hollingsworth was accused of multiple bigamy he excused himself on the grounds that one of these previous wives had been no wife at all. The woman, Susannah Belling, according to his testimony, 'knowing her infirmity ought not to have married; her infirmity is such that no man can lie with her, and because it is so she has ways with women . . . which is not fit to be named but most rank whorish they are . . .'

Some women dressed as men in order to make money. Anthony Wood, an Oxford antiquarian, described in a letter of 1694 how one young woman had appeared at the King's Bench in male apparel where she 'was found guilty of marrying a young maid, whose portion she had obtained and was very nigh of being contracted of a second marriage'. Her letters to other projected wives were read out in court, to much laughter, and she was sentenced 'to be well whipped and kept to hard labour'.

In 1695, as recorded in a pamphlet with the title of *The*

Counterfeit Bridegroom, a lady of Southwark advertised a dowry of £200 for any eligible suitor for her daughter. There must have been a crowd of young men tempted by such bait, but the young lady herself chose 'a young smock-faced pretended youth, lately arrived from Ireland, under the disguised name of Mr K, a squire's son'. In truth he was a she. As soon as they were in bed, the fraud was discovered; but not until Mr K had escaped with the dowry. Another kind of speculation came to light in the summer of 1701 when, according to *The English Post*, 'a woman, in the habit of a man, was lately seized at Soho in the act of coining and was sent to Newgate'. A similar financial speculation was recorded in a London prison list of 1720 where Sarah Ketson, calling herself John, tried to inveigle Ann Hutchinson into marriage.

The funereal monument of Katherine Bovey was raised in Westminster Abbey after her death in 1727. According to its inscription the memorial was at the behest of Mary Pope 'who lived with her near forty years in perfect friendship'. More interestingly, it has been plausibly suggested that Katherine Bovey was the model of 'the perverse widow' in the *Spectator* of 1711 who delighted in luring on passionate bachelors only to reject their suits at the last moment. Richard Steele wrote that 'this perverse woman is one of those unaccountable creatures that secretly rejoice in the admiration of men, but indulge themselves in no further consequences'. He added, with no attempt at irony, that 'she is always accompanied by a confidante, who is witness to her daily protestations against our sex'. One of those confidantes may have been Mary Pope.

Riley Pinx.
R.W. sc.
Mrs. Behn.
Vol. I.
Pa. 29.

9

Suck thy master

Many trysting places for males could be found in seventeenth-century London. Saffron Hill, south of Clerkenwell and close to Cowcross Street, was always worth a visit. The courtyards and alleys of Clerkenwell itself were interesting; Field Lane was one of its more notorious venues. 'I am ruined, for ever ruined!' one of the characters in John Dryden's *The Wild Gallant* (1663) laments. 'Plague, had you no places to name in town but Sodom and Lucknor's Lane for lodgings!' 'Sodom' may have been the brothel close to the Whitefriars Theatre, while Lewknors Lane, as it was properly called, off Drury Lane, may have had a similar reputation. As the city progressed to the west, however, so did the centres of sex move with it to Vauxhall and to the newly established 'West End'. The Fountain Tavern, a public house just off the Strand, was one example. Dick's Coffee House in Aldersgate, and the Pheasant in Fuller's Rents, Holborn, were well known for their special clientele. They were not alone. There were probably as many 'gay bars', in terms of population, in seventeenth- as in twenty-first-century London.

The Royal Exchange in the City, with its arcades and quiet corners for trade, had been a haunt ever since its inception; towards the end of the century the *London Spy* described how a group of sightseers 'went on the 'Change, turned to the right, and jostled in amongst a parcel of swarthy buggerantoes, preter-natural fornicators, as my friend called them, who would ogle a handsome young man with as much lust as a true-bred

English whoremaster would gaze upon a beautiful woman'. In the middle of the seventeenth century a 'spintry', or male brothel, was established in the Mulberry Garden, on the present site of Buckingham Palace. The prostitutes were often paid with clothes rather than money. A contemporary list of 'common whores' included some male names, among them Little Taffy, Dick Steckwel, Ned Brooks and Ralph Asbington, also known as 'Shittern-arse'. Five 'beastly sodomitical boys' embarked on the crossing over the Atlantic in 1629, no doubt ready to ply their trade in the New World; but they were caught in the act and sent back to England.

Anyone in a public space was fair game. The aisles of St Paul's Cathedral, as well as St Paul's Churchyard, were honey traps. The secluded alley to the north of the Chapter House was a particular favourite. 'Sodomites' Walk' on Upper Moorfields was obviously well named. Others were attracted to the dark river, where the various dank and dirty lanes running into Shadwell or Limehouse fostered good trade in seamen seeking male prostitutes or men in search of sailors. Men might lounge against the pillars of Covent Garden market, or they might make frequent visits to the public toilets of Lincoln's Inn Fields, Moorfields and Green Park. In fact the latrines of any park would do; trees, grass and bushes stirred the blood. In John Ford's *The Lover's Melancholy* (1628) a male servant, dressed as a female and called Lady Periwinkle, is enjoined to 'suck thy master'; the primary meaning was 'suckle', but the other meanings were known.

A contemporary records that 'if one of them sits upon a bench he pats the back of his hands; if you follow them, they put a white handkerchief through the skirts of the coat, and wave it to and fro; but if they are met by you, their thumbs are stuck in the armpits of their waistcoats, and they play their

Greek red figure pottery (*c.* 480–323 BC) with idealised males in various erotic poses.

A Saxon chieftain, part of a rich and homo-erotic culture. The men dressed more extravagantly than the women.

An image of London under Roman domination. A statue of the military emperor, Trajan, who is believed to have been exclusively gay, close to the remains of the Roman bathhouse at Billingsgate on what is now Lower Thames Street.

London Bridge delineated by Claes Visscher (1586–1652) in the early seventeenth century. Its lavatories were well known sites for queer assignations.

William II or William Rufus, well known for creating a gay court and promoting orgies with young men.

The murder of Piers Gaveston. Gaveston was bitterly resented because of his extraordinary closeness to Edward II, which had all the appearance of a sexual union.

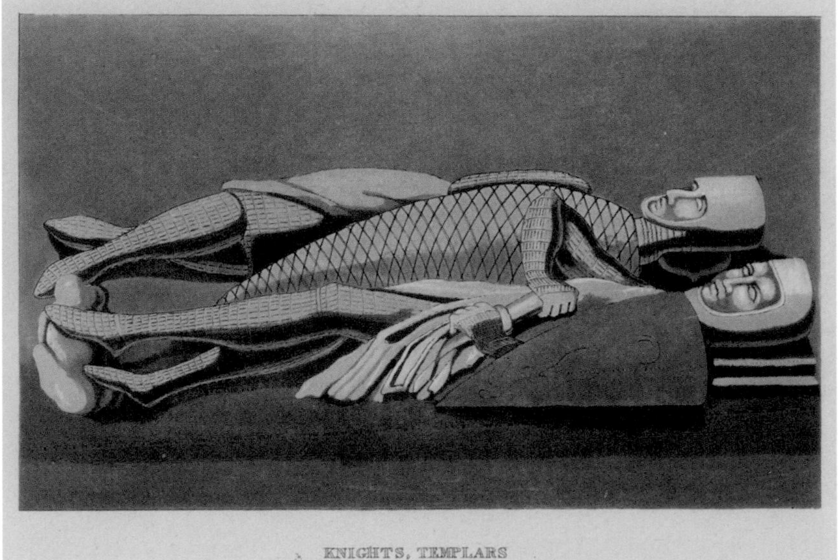

The joint effigy of two Knights Templar. The Templars were regularly accused of sodomy and related sexual practices, and were banished from the kingdom.

From William Blake's engraving of the Canterbury pilgrims on their way out of London. Chaucer provides two of the first descriptions of London queers, the Pardoner and the Summoner.

A map of London before the Great Fire. Certain divines and moralists blamed the conflagration on the prevalence of sodomy among the clerisy and nobility of the city.

Shakespeare treated sodomy as a natural thing, and his eighteenth sonnet is a love poem that seems to be addressed to a man. Of course he also made full use of the theatrical convention whereby boys dressed as women on the stage. But he was of so fluid and mercurial a temper that the matter is undecided.

Christopher Marlowe's most famous remark, 'all they that love not tobacco and boys are fools', was accredited to him by a government agent but it has survived as a permanent clue to his sexual identity.

James I of England and James VI of Scotland, a notorious devotee of gay sex. He was known to slobber over his favourites and to one of them, the Duke of Buckingham, he wrote that: 'I desire only to live in this world, for your sake … I had rather live banished in any part of the world with you, than live a sorrowful widow's life without you … god bless you my sweet child & wife & grant that you may ever be a comfort to your dear dad and husband.' It was said that King Elizabeth had been succeeded by Queen James.

A panorama of swashbuckling females who preferred to live on the wild side

Ann Mills, who dressed as a dragoon to serve on the *Maidstone* frigate in 1740. She lived and, apparently, killed as a man.

Christina Davies enlisted under the name of Christopher Welsh and served in many campaigns under the Duke of Marlborough.

Mary Ann Talbot ran the gamut of naval occupations as drummer, powder monkey, cabin boy and steward.

Ann Bonny and Mary Read were convicted of piracy in 1720; their apparent courage and solidarity nevertheless won them many admirers, not all of them male.

'A Morning Frolic, or the Transmutation of Sexes' (*c.* 1780) is a satire upon the cross-dressing of the sexes which had a licentious appeal to those who wished to transgress.

A 'molly' is pilloried after being caught *in flagrante*. The aggression of the London mob was well known, and many of these victims died or were severely injured at its hands.

The great boy actor Edward Kynaston (1640–1712) who captured the hearts and minds (and other organs) of fashionable audiences.

William III, who had invaded England in 1688. Another great queer military leader, his amours with his Dutch commanders were matters of popular satire.

fingers upon their breasts'. They wore Italian short cloaks to emphasise their buttocks.

The gestures of the hands were important. If the middle finger was advanced, it was a sign of effeminacy. The hand turned up, in the course of conversation, was another token. So, unusually enough, was the act of scratching the head with one finger. If you 'wagged' your hand as you walked, it was a sign of sodomitical shamelessness; it was a completely unnecessary, and therefore wanton, gesture. This may be the first example of what became known as the 'swishy' gay.

A servant, Meredith Davy, had the habit of taking to his bed one of his master's young apprentices by the name of John Vincent; he limited himself to Sundays and holidays, after he had been drinking. But he did not do so in privacy and seclusion; another servant shared the bedchamber and could clearly hear the sounds of sexual activity; the bed creaked and the boy groaned. When the servant eventually gave evidence to that effect, at his prosecution in 1630, the reaction of the defendant was bewilderment. It had not occurred to him that he was doing anything particularly wrong. Perhaps it was the custom of the county. He said in his defence only that 'he denieth that he ever used any unclean action with the said boy as they lay in bed together; and more he sayeth not'. He was not charged, and went back to the same sleeping arrangements as before. Why would he engage in intercourse with the boy in front of a witness? Why did he deny any uncleanliness? Did the combination of drunkenness and Sundays or holidays make it somehow acceptable, a kind of ritual practice? Meredith Davy would no doubt have flatly denied that he was a sodomite, and he would have been readily believed.

The case of Mervyn Touchet, earl of Castlehaven, was quite different. In 1630 his son, James, complained about his father's unnatural behaviour with the young servants of the house; he claimed that his father committed sodomy and buggery and, at the subsequent Privy Council investigation, three pages and a footman confessed to congress not only with the earl but with the earl's wife and daughter-in-law. It all became very messy. Audley and two of the servants were hanged on the charges of rape and sodomy. His gravest sin, however, was to threaten the stability of the patriarchal household; all his crimes and sins were rolled together as a danger to social order. He had to go.

The execution of Charles I, and the subsequent quasi-monarchical reign of Oliver Cromwell, may conceivably have cast a pall on the more obvious signs of urban queerness. The theatres, for example, were closed down in 1642. A few illicit productions were still staged in private houses, but much of the gaiety had gone. All was changed with the restoration of Charles II. We read of a new tavern for ingles, the Three Potters, in Cripplegate Without, thriving by 1661. And the theatres were open once more. The boy actors returned and one of them, Edward Kynaston, became the darling of the age. Buggery was once again in fashion, even if perhaps more delicately handled than in the time of James I. The merry monarch did not mind what came to be known as mollies.

Kynaston specialised in female parts and as such he obtained many male admirers who were more interested in his own parts. He was described at the time as 'a complete stage beauty', even though female actors themselves were now permitted on the stage. In his diary Pepys describes him as 'the loveliest lady that ever I saw in my life'. One of his lovers, according to London rumour, was George Villiers, 2nd Duke of Buckingham, who was a favourite of the king. One contemporary satire remarks that 'Kenaston's arse knows its own buggerer' while Buckingham is described 'with Kenaston acting both Venus and Mars'. In his old age Kynaston recalled the time when he was 'so beautiful a youth' that the fashionable ladies 'prided themselves in taking him with them in their coaches to Hyde Park, in his theatrical habit [costume], after the play'. It seems, however, that it was not only the ladies whom he entertained. Buckingham himself enjoyed masculine as well as feminine attentions but, according to one report of the court of Charles II, he particularly relished the 'most rascally lackeys' or male servants.

The Wandering Whore (1660), already marked out as the setting for lesbian pornography, laments the fact that male customers who attended brothels 'had rather be dealing with smooth-faced 'prentices'. It also provides one of the few descriptions of an effeminate male in this period. 'There likewise hermaphrodites, effeminate men, men given to much luxury, idleness and wanton pleasures, and to that abominable sin of sodomy, wherein they are both active and passive in it, whose vicious actions are only to be whispered amongst us.'

Another cross-dressing actor who graced or disgraced the Restoration stage, James 'Nursery' Nokes, was a victim of suspicion and innuendo. He is one of the subjects of the *Satyr on the Players* (1682), where unwitting apprentices are asked to:

> Secure your gentle bums
> For full of lust and fury see he comes!
> 'Tis buggering Nokes, whose damned unwieldy tarse
> Weeps to be buried in his foreman's arse,
> Unnatural sinner, lecher without sense,
> To leave kind cunt to dive in excrements.

A further insight into the Restoration court is furnished by an entry in Pepys's diary. In the summer of 1663 one of the more notable courtiers, Sir Charles Sedley, went naked onto the balcony of the Cock Inn in Bow Street where with a companion he acted out 'all the postures of lust and buggery that could be imagined'. (An anonymous song of the period records that 'Sedley has fuck't a thousand arses'.) Pepys then records the subsequent conversation at a dinner party when two naval officials 'both say that buggery is now grown almost as common among our gallants as in Italy, and that the very pages of the town begin to complain of their masters for it. But blessed be God I do not to this day know what is the meaning of this sin, nor which is the agent nor which the patient.' The sense of an earlier entry in the diary, for 15 August 1660, is therefore open to interpretation. Pepys was in his chamber with a colleague 'with whom I did intend to lie; but he and I fell to play with one another, so that I made him go lie with Mr Shaply, So I lay alone all night.' They were clearly not playing cards.

Pepys observed the women as well as the men. In the summer of 1666 he was at Whitehall where 'I find the ladies of honour dressed in their riding garbs, with coats and doublets with deep skirts, just for all the world like men, and buttoned their doublets up the breast, with periwigs and with hats; so that, only for a long petticoat dragging under their men's coats nobody could take them for women in any point whatever'. It was a queer world.

In 1668 the first play by a woman that celebrates female eroticism, as well as female transvestism, was composed. *The Convent of Pleasure* by Margaret Cavendish, Duchess of Newcastle, concerns a group of women who flee from a world of males to enjoy each other in their own cloistered nook. A great foreign princess, described as 'a princely brave woman truly, of a masculine presence', begins what can only be described as an affair with Lady Happy. Some strong sentiments follow. Lady Happy has a question. 'But why may not I love a woman with the same affection as a man?' A few lines later the princess 'of a masculine mind' replies 'nay, it were a sin in friendship, should we not kiss'. The stage direction reveals that 'they embrace and kiss, and hold each other in their arms'. Female eroticism had come out into the open.

The poet of Restoration London was undoubtedly John Wilmot, Earl of Rochester, who led a profane and reckless career at court under the usually benevolent eye of the king. Rochester knew all the vices of London, and could begin with the trees and bushes of St James's Park: 'And nightly now beneath their shade / Are buggeries, rapes and incests made.'

He sent his French page to a close friend, Henry Savile, with the message that 'the greatest and gravest of this court of both sexes have tasted his beauties'.

Rochester is also presumed to be the author of a fantastical farce entitled *Sodom, or the Quintessence of Debauchery* (1684) in which the king of Sodom issues a proclamation in favour of sodomy:

> I do proclaim that bugg'ry may be us'd
> Through all the land, so cunt be not abus'd . . .
> To Buggeranthus let this charge be given,
> And let them bugger all things under heaven.

His own motto is 'I'll reign and bugger still!' The women protest, claiming that they are better lovers because they are insatiable, and the curtain comes down on scenes of fire and brimstone as the king calls out in defiance:

> Let Heavens descend and set the world on fire!
> We to some darker cavern will retire;
> There on thy buggered arse I will expire.

Rochester became a little more serious in his tragedy *Valentinian* (1685), where the emperor tells the eunuch:

> Oh let me press these balmy lips all day,
> And bathe my love-scorched soul in thy moist kisses.

Rochester's poem to his supposed mistress was far less sentimental:

> When each the well-looked link boy strove t'enjoy,
> And the best kiss was the deciding lot
> Whether the boy fucked you, or I the boy.

Link boys, who held lights to aid pedestrians at night, were well known for their readiness to provide other favours.

Boys did indeed seem to become an endangered species. A pamphlet of 1669, entitled the *Children's Petition*, was directed against unmitigated flogging and its attendant practices. The 'children' state that 'our sufferings are of that nature as makes our schools to be not merely houses of correction, but of prostitution, in this vile way of castigation in use, wherein our secret parts which are by nature shameful and not to be uncovered, must be the anvil exposed to the immodest eyes, and filthy blows of the smiter'. The schoolmaster whipped the buttocks of the boy because they were the source of his temptation and sin, but they may have excited the posterior for further action. The pamphlet concludes that 'if the nation will not take the warning, but will be wicked, and a Sodom, let it be wicked still'.

It was believed that too much beating in boyhood led inexorably to adult vice and as Ned Ward put it in the *London Spy*

(1703), those 'in the black-school of sodomy are call'd by learned students in the science of debauchery, flogging-cullies'. The 'flogging cully' was supposed to be an old rogue or fool who liked to whip or be whipped. Judging by the references in fiction and drama there must have been many such 'cullies', but the historical and judicial records bear little trace of their presence. They were part of the unknown aspect of queer London. They were perhaps part of its mythology.

A case came before the magistrates of the Old Bailey in the winter of 1667, where an apprentice of fifteen years had been accused of running away from his master. But the boy spoke out and said, in the words of the transcript, 'that his said master, Thomas Rivers, did one time when his mistress was forth, invite him the said Henry Wells into bed to him and asked if he were cold, which he said he was, and then and there he buggered him, and entered his body; and after that he took him in the cellar, and tied him up by the two wrists, and there abused him; and also that upon a Sunday after, the said master took him out into the fields, and did the like unto him after he had bound him'. He swore that he had been buggered eight times. But he was lying. His mother had coached him in his testimony, and she was seen to whisper to him whenever he was interrogated. When the halter was put around the neck of Thomas Rivers at Tyburn, the boy cried out that he had wronged his master and sworn falsely against him. Rivers was saved at the last moment. There is no moral to this story, except for the fact that it was relatively easy to lay a false charge of sodomy.

Foreigners, who were thought to swarm through the London streets, were always suspect. Lorenzo in Aphra Behn's play *The Amorous Prince* (1671) remarks to himself that ''tis a fine lad, how plump and white he is; would I could meet him somewhere i' th' dark, I'd have a fling at him, and try whether I were right Florentine'. He asks the boy how long he had 'been set up for thyself', plying his trade as a prostitute; he tells him not to chase women because it will 'spoil a good face and mar your better market of the two'. John Dryden's *An Evening's Love* (1668) made a similar allusion:

MASKALL: I imagined them to be Italians.
LOPEZ: Not unlikely, for they played most furiously at our backsides.

Sodomy could also be blamed on the French as well as the Italians. In his epilogue to *The Duke of Guise* (1683), Dryden described sex between men as 'a damned love-trick new brought over from France' in which men 'club for love'; this suggests specific meeting places rather than the walking of streets or parks. The name for participants was often 'Neuters'. John Vanbrugh's *The Relapse* (1696) has the virtue of presenting the first fully formed English queer on the London stage.

COUPLER: Ha, you young lascivious rogue, you! Let me put my hand in your bosom, sirrah!
FASHION: Stand off, old Sodom!

Yet some odd couples still managed to achieve a monumental stillness. Two men can stand beside each other in funereal statuary. A memorial of 1619 in Gonville and Caius, Cambridge, celebrates the union between Thomas Legge and John Gostlin; it displays a heart in flames with a Latin inscription which, translated, reads 'Love joined them living. So may the earth join them in their burial. O Legge, Gostlin's heart you have still with you.' A monument of 1684 to John Finch and Thomas Baines in the chapel of Christ's College,

Cambridge, contains a knotted cloth in token of the *connubium*, or marriage, between the two men. These memorials, between men and men or women and women, have already been noted from previous centuries. Yet they continued well into the early modern period and are an indication that even the established Church spotted no fault in these unusual same-sex relationships.

Capt. Edward Rigby of
Leyton in Lanci-shire
T. Murray pinx.
1702 I. Smith fec.

10

Arsey-Versy

In 1691 the Society for the Reformation of Manners began its activities, some of them designed to put an end to the 'scourge' of sodomy that was said to have polluted the streets of London. It was assisted by a subtle change in the law with the new charge of 'assault with intent to commit unnatural crimes'; if one man 'laid hands' on another, he could be accused of assaulting him.

These measures were in part derived from a rise of public consciousness concerning what became known as 'molly houses', havens in which queer men could meet and drink, dance with each other, and bugger each other, with what they considered to be impunity. In this they were mistaken.

The references to same-sex love among males may have been heated by rumours about the new king, William III, who had been given the crown in 1689. He was a successful military commander who, among other feats, had hustled James II from the throne; but many successful soldiers were known for their interest in sodomy. William himself had been attached to William Bentinck, ennobled as the Earl of Portland, and the gossip about the two men reached the public in satires and ballads. The king was accused of buggering Bentinck and the favourite was called a 'catamite who rules alone the state' or, more unusually, a 'bardash' or the equivalent of the French '*bardache*', meaning man-woman or passive male prostitute. One satire put it this way:

In love to his minions he partial and rash is,
Makes statesmen of blockheads and earls of bardashes.

When the king seems to have transferred his affections to another Dutchman, Arnold Joost van Keppel, Bentinck threw up all his public offices in a fit of pique. William remonstrated with him, and Bentinck replied that 'the kindness which your majesty shows to a young man and the manner in which you appear to authorize his liberties and impertinencies make the world say things I am ashamed to hear'. The king's friend, Bishop Burnet, remarked in his *History of His Own Time* (1723) that William 'had no vice, but of one sort, in which he was very cautious and secret', to which Swift responded in a marginal handwritten entry that 'it was of two sorts – *male* and *female* – in the *former* he was neither cautious nor secret'.

In a later supplement to the *History*, Burnet concluded that 'if he has been guilty of any of the disorders that are too common to princes, yet he has not practiced them as some to whom he is nearly related have done, but has endeavoured to cover them; though let princes be as secret as they will in such matters, they are always known'. He wrote only one more thing of relevance in his supplement. He alluded to 'another particular, that is too tender to put in writing' which might affect the king's reputation.

Charles Spencer, 3rd Earl of Sunderland, was also the victim of much rumour. A Scottish reverend, Robert Wodrow, lamented in his diary the prevalence in London of 'the abomination of sodomy'. He went on to say that 'the earl of Sunderland was the first who set up houses for that vile sin, and when this was like to break out, poisoned himself, to prevent the discovery'. A packet of letters was published in 1723 with the title of *Love-Letters Between a Certain late*

Nobleman and the Famous Beau Wilson. Wilson was an army captain, as handsome as he was vain, who in 1693 was overflowing with money from some mysterious patron. In one copy of the *Love-Letters*, now in the British Library, a written entry identifies this 'late Nobleman' as the Earl of Sunderland who had died a year before its publication. The last document of this case has the name of *The Conspirators: Or, The Case of Catiline* (1721), written by 'Britannicus' and dedicated to Sunderland. It alludes to a sodomitical club, catering to higher ministers and courtiers, some of whom dressed as women for their visits; this would indeed be described as a 'conspiracy' at the time, but, if it did exist, any other evidence for it has disappeared. The *Love-Letters* may have been entirely a work of fiction and several identifications of the 'late Nobleman' have been suggested. The whole episode might mean anything or nothing. But it does at least bear witness to the overheated sexual atmosphere of the time. A letter to the Duke of Shrewsbury from James Vernon, secretary of state, written at this time of moral outrage among Londoners, claimed that 'the City as well as the Court is full of such sparks, and that they are all in the offices'; by which he meant the offices of state. Could it be that, for a while, the country was run by a cabal of queers?

The wife of one of the king's most notoriously queer relations, 'Monsieur' or the Duke of Orléans, had no doubt about the English attachment to same-sex unions. The duchess, Liselotte, wrote that the new English king had no fondness for women and 'he is believed to have very different inclinations'; he was part of 'that brotherhood' and in the year before his death she wrote of those men 'who share the inclinations of king William'. She was once asked whether the English court had become a '*château de derrière*', or arse castle. She added that 'nothing is more ordinary in England than this unnatural vice'. For England, she meant London.

An anonymous writer posing as a procuress and brothel-keeper, 'Jenny Cromwell', composed a pamphlet entitled *Jenny Cromwell's Complaint Against Sodomy* (1692) which associated the London court with its queer inhabitants. Among the elite circle of the sodomites she mentioned 'Bardash' or Bentinck and the king; another candidate for inclusion was the Earl of Scarsdale who was wont 'to skulk about the alleys / And is content with Bettys, Nans and Mollys'. 'Jenny Cromwell' rose to a final condemnation against William III: 'Till you came in and with your Reformation / Turn'd all things Arsy Versey in the Nation.'

James Stanhope, one day destined to become another earl, entered the House of Commons in 1701 at the start of an illustrious career both as soldier and statesman. But the stories about him were already circulating and in 1703 a satirical squib named him as one 'Who thinks no pleasure like Italian joy / And to a Venus arms prefers a pathic boy'. In the same year the Earl of Huntingdon wrote to him from Paris pledging friendship. 'What would I not give you to tell you this my wicked Stanhope over a glass of champagne in Paris with two or three pretty smiling unthinking fellows that know nothing and do everything.'

Another bevy of courtiers were accused:

> Thinking they must be mimics to the crown
> They to each other put their breeches down
> If Wentworth one of these with bum will bless
> He's not a little proud of his success.

Thomas Wentworth was an intimate of the king. It might seem that everybody was doing it. At a later date, a general in the

British Army, Sir John Cope, was believed to have earned his promotion as a result of his 'prolific bum'.

The temperature of the time was further raised with the case of Captain Edward Rigby. On 5 November 1698 Rigby approached a young man, William Minton, nineteen years old, in St James's Park where the youth had gone to watch the firework display; he squeezed the boy's hand before taking out his erect penis and giving it to him to fondle; then he kissed the boy, and put his tongue in his mouth. The boy ran off but Rigby caught up with him; they arranged an assignation for two days later in the George Tavern on Pall Mall. He was to ask for 'number four'. But Minton, having changed his mind about this tryst, informed his master who in turn approached Thomas Bray, a representative of the Society for the Reformation of Manners. This was the kind of opportunity for which the members of the society yearned. It may even have been Bray who set up the trap.

It was laid for Rigby in the George. The constables, in hiding until the moment of arrest, overheard Rigby trying to lure the boy. He raised a toast to him, he kissed him, and pushed the boy's hand into his breeches. Then the captain sat on the boy's lap and kissed him some more.

'Should I fuck you?' Rigby asked him.

'How can that be?' Minton asked him.

'I'll show you, for it is no more than was done in our forefathers' time.' He cited some eminent examples, including a French king and a Russian tsar, before uttering 'most blasphemous words' no doubt concerning Christ and his favourite disciple. He embraced and kissed Minton again and confessed that 'his lust was provoked' to the point where he had ejaculated in his breeches. But he was still ready for more and took Minton into a corner where he took down his breeches and stuck his finger into Minton's 'fundament'. He then put his erect penis against the boy and in his testimony Minton stated that 'feeling something warm touch his skin, put his hand behind him and took hold of Rigby's privy member'.

The time had come. Minton made for the door, stamped his foot on the floor and called out 'Westminster!' This was the code word to alert the constables, who now rushed into the room and arrested Rigby. At the eventual trial the judges found Rigby guilty of the heinous crime of sodomy; he was fined one thousand pounds, given a year's imprisonment, and consigned to the pillories at Pall Mall, Charing Cross and Temple Bar on three successive days between eleven and one. The last punishments might have been the worst, since the pillory was sometimes a death sentence. But Rigby had friends in high places. He dressed as a beau and was required only to stand beside the pillory and not to be held down by it; he was also surrounded by constables and beadles to ensure that no interested bystander could throw anything at him. Conveniently he escaped from confinement and absconded to France.

It was not unusual for boys or young men to be propositioned in this manner, especially in London. In the same month of 1698 Richard Kirby made a play for his barber's servant, Joseph Thomas. When the boy went down into the cellar, for the purposes of nature, Kirby followed him to indulge in a bout of mutual masturbation. He then asked Thomas to turn his back, but when the boy refused, he 'put a finger up his fundament and the nail of his finger under the foreskin of his yard'. The operation may not have been entirely satisfactory since in the spring of the following year Kirby tried again. He took out the boy's penis and then masturbated himself until 'he spent his nature on the boards'; still he was not satisfied and he put his penis between the legs of the boy 'and rubbed himself until he spent his seed into [Thomas's] breeches'. The boy made a formal complaint on 16 June, but the case was not brought to trial. It was lost in the turmoil of London. Sexual assaults upon children were both more common and more disregarded than in the twenty-first century.

11

Continually wet

By the beginning of the eighteenth century the queer culture of London was coming under more sustained attack than before. The notion of the effeminate homosexual was now prevalent. A play of 1703, Thomas Baker's *Tunbridge-Walks*, satirises the queer coxcombs in the delicate shape of Mr Maiden describing his acquaintance.

> Oh! The best creatures in the World; we have such diversion, when we meet together at my chambers. There's Beau Simper, Beau Rabbitsface, Beau Eithersex, Colonel Coachpole, and Count Drivel, that sits with his mouth open . . . Then we never read Gazettes nor talk of Venlo and Vigo [battles], like your coffee-house fellows; but play with fans, and mimic the women, scream, hold up our tails, make curtsies, and call one another, Madam . . .

Many of them went around London 'strolling and caterwauling' or, in other words, looking for sex. Such a man would talk of fans and masques and pretty gloves; he understood as much about silk and ribbons as any milliner, and knew all about beauty washes and the essences of perfume. That, at least, was the popular image.

An article, under the assumed name of 'Mrs Crackenthorpe' (aka Thomas Baker) in the *Female Tatler* of 1709, records the conversation of a milliner on Ludgate Hill. 'This, madame, is wonderful charming. This, madame, is so diverting a silk. This, madame – my stars! How cool it looks.' Mrs Crackenthorpe bids only ten shillings a yard. 'Fan me you winds, your ladyship rallies me! Should I part with it at such a price, the weavers would rise upon the very shop! Was you at the park last night, madame? Your ladyship shall abate me sixpence. Have you read the *Tatler* today?' Et cetera.

Joseph Addison wrote in 1711 of a young gentleman who is 'a wonderful critic in cambric and muslins, and will talk an hour together upon a sweet-meat'. (It might be mentioned that Alexander Pope described Addison and Steele as 'a couple of hermaphrodites', which meant no more than that they were queer. The suggestion cannot be confirmed.) In Frances Burney's *Evelina* (1778), the heroine scorns male milliners as 'so finical! So affected! They seemed to understand every part of a woman's dress better that we do ourselves; and they recommend caps and ribbons with an air of such importance, that I wished to ask them how long they had left off wearing them!'

It was generally acknowledged that certain places of public resort were of interest to the queers of London. A German traveller, Zacharias von Uffenbach, noted 'the great quantity of Moors . . . hawking their bottoms round the Strand and Covent Garden'. Among other favoured spots were the 'houses of office' available in taverns or inns. The 'bog-houses' of Savoy, the Temple and Lincoln's Inn Fields were also popular. Holes were sometimes made in the partitions to facilitate intimacy. The *London Post* of 20 June 1701 reported that 'on Thursday, between 10 and 11 at night, a person sitting in Lincolns-Inn house of office, a young man happened to go into the same box, whom the other welcomed, and afterwards entered into a discourse with him, pretending great kindness for him etcetera. But at last discovered his intention, to commit the filthy sin of sodomy with him, and made an attempt to force him. But the young man crying out, some of the porters and watchmen of the Inn, as well as some of the young gentlemen, came to his assistance and soon cooled the spark's courage, by ducking him in the said house of office, and afterwards left him to shift for himself.'

Such enclaves were generally known as 'the markets' where men might 'pick up trade'. The language of commerce, so vital to London in this period, had entered the speech of the streets. To be involved in casual sex was 'to bite a blow' after 'making a bargain', while a male prostitute might 'put the bite' on a customer. That could include blackmail, extortion or physical violence. The members of the Society for the Reformation of Manners were of course interested in these transactions, and their agents went to great lengths to snare and entrap the unwary. Those who were caught faced the prospect of fines, or imprisonment, or a ducking in the Thames almost until death, or the pillory set up wherever they had been caught in the act.

As a result of the work of the society's secret agents, several men were convicted, among them a foot soldier named Thomas Lane. He is supposed to have come up to Mr Hemmings, no doubt a good-looking decoy, and 'pulling out his nakedness offer'd to put it into his hand, and withal unbutton'd the evidence's [witness's] breeches'. In his defence Lane stated that 'he had been at St Thomas's Hospital, and coming over the bridge, he went to make water, and that the evidence's hand slipped upon his nakedness'. Other men were caught on similar charges, some of whom committed suicide while detained in prison.

There are several cases where a man's 'naked yard' is displayed and put in the hands of another, while on certain occasions there were forcible attempts to enter the breeches of the supposed victim. There was little subtlety about it, but rather a great deal of assertion and aggressiveness which may give some indication of the general state of sexuality in eighteenth-century London. It was not a period of extended foreplay or romance. Such forcible practices may often have been successful; perhaps the perpetrator did not believe that his victim would go to a magistrate, where the risk of a counter-charge might have been great; but it had always been the manner of the London streets, where violence was endemic. William Oliver, for example, wrestled William Sidall to the ground before he thrust his hand into Oliver's breeches and pulled out his sensitive parts. John Blair encountered Samuel Beakley in Sudney's Alley late at night but then assaulted him when Beakley could not be coerced to entertain Blair's 'sodomitical practices'.

The consequences of public disclosure, however, were very severe. The parish clerk of St Dunstan's in the East committed suicide by cutting his own throat after being accused of an 'unnatural crime'. Henry Thorp hanged himself from a tree in St George's Fields after being confronted by blackmailers. It was wise to be cautious. Men no longer kissed one another in the old fashion, the embrace gradually being replaced by the more formal handshake. The intimacy of lips was now considered to be the preserve of foreigners. 'I love to kiss a man,' a character says in Colley Cibber's *Love Makes a Man; or, The Fop's Fortune* (1700). 'In Paris, we kiss nothing else.' To shake hands was to create an informal contract, much more agreeable to the mercantile middle class than false fondness.

Yet even though kissing was now generally regarded as the first station of Sodom, some fops or rakes persisted. 'Ah, my Georgy! Kiss!' Lord Wronglove exclaims to Sir George Brilliant in Cibber's *The Lady's Last Stake* (1707). 'And kiss and kiss again, my dear,' Brilliant replies. 'By Ganymede here's nectar on thy lips. O the pleasure of a friend to tell the joy. O Wronglove! Such hopes!' So such matters were aired on the stage to general amusement. The 'camp' comedian, to use a relatively modern phrase, is almost as old as the city itself. A gay harlequinade was staged as early as 1702 when the 'Mard Brothers' performed a 'night piece'. 'What ridiculous postures and grimaces,' one contemporary wrote, 'and seeming in labour with a monstrous birth, at last my counterfeit male lady is delivered of her two puppets, Harlequin and Scaramouch.' No doubt those 'postures and grimaces' were performed in the best possible taste.

There were dangers other than those of arrest and punishment. In John Marten's *A Treatise of all the Degrees and Symptoms of the Venereal Disease, in both Sexes* (1709), it was revealed that 'the distemper' may be contracted 'by a man's putting his erected penis into another person's (man's or woman's) mouth using friction etcetera between the lips'. One of Marten's informants told him that 'it was with great pleasure that he ejected it into the person's mouth he had to do with, who willingly received it, and assisted, as he said, in this foul act, by sucking his penis'. At a slightly later date it was known as 'gamahuching', from the French. Marten also described in some detail other venereal infections, such as gonorrhoea, which had spread through queer London.

This was also the period when the 'molly houses' came fully into public view. Clubs for queer men were not unusual in any period of London's history, but at the beginning of the eighteenth century they became the object of sensational pamphlets and periodicals. Before that date they had generally been tolerated or ignored, part of the great forgetfulness of London; they might even have been admired by those citizens who followed the London radical tradition of paying tribute to rebels and insurgents of any description. Now all was changed. In 1702 a pamphlet was issued under the title of *The Sodomites' Shame and Doom: Laid Before Them with Great Grief and Compassion by a Minister of the Church of England*. The 'compassion' was in short supply; the 'minister' – representative as he was of the Church of England – warned that 'your names and places of abode are known' and were at risk of 'being visited by such as may bring your crimes to just punishment'. The punishment in question was 'the gallows, which our laws have justly appointed to your sin'.

The increased interest provided a welcome opportunity for the blackmailer who could now fall into the company of an unsuspecting gentleman before accusing him of attempted buggery. Sometimes this worked, and sometimes it did not. Soldiers became expert blackmailers; they seemed to be readily available, but they could easily be rough. Groups of them were known to haunt St James's Park, a well-known spot for the military, and they were ready to come to one another's aid at the call of 'Stop, sodomite!' Any man, blameless or otherwise, might find himself helpless in the face of their demands; money, and clothes, and valuables, passed from hand to hand. Birdcage Walk was considered to be unusually dangerous.

The victim might be fortunate, however. In a trial of February 1708 at the Old Bailey, it was revealed that William Hollis, while walking along the Strand, had asked George Skelthorp the way to King Street. Skelthorp agreed to take him there 'but instead of that conducted him to a private place, where was a horse-pond but dried up, and there took him by the collar, demanding satisfaction. Saying he was a sodomite, and drawing his bayonet offered it at his breast, took from him four shillings and sixpence, pulled off his coat, and was endeavouring to get off his rings, but was prevented by some people coming up, who hearing him [Hollis] beg for his life, came to his assistance, and seized the prisoner with the coat and money upon him.'

Skelthorp was a practised blackmailer. At his subsequent trial he confessed that he knew the times and places 'where some sodomites were resorting about Covent Garden, he went to stand in their way, and when any of them would (as they often did) carry him to a by-place thereabouts to commit their foul acts with him, he went with them; and then he, taking hold of them, threatened them, that he would presently bring them before a justice, unless they gave him satisfaction'. So they gave him money, rings and watches 'or what else they had then about them'.

In 1707 a 'sodomites' club' in the City was raided, while a number of known trysting places such as London Bridge and the arcades of the Royal Exchange were systematically invaded. A favourite spot was Pope's Head Alley just by the Exchange. One agent, Thomas Vauhan, loitered in the Strand and Covent Garden in search of victims he might entrap. One man who was caught, a porter, William Huggins, said after his arrest that 'he had heard there were such sort of persons in the world, and he had a mind to try'. Another man was arrested for 'frigging', or masturbating.

The net had been set by the Society for the Reformation of Manners. In earlier years there had only been one or two individual cases, generally involving a breach of the peace rather than any particular accusation. A pamphlet of 1707, John Dunton's *The He-Strumpets: A Satire on the Sodomite Club*, could now boast that there had been forty arrests and three suicides; those who had killed themselves were a merchant, a draper and a curate, two of them hanging themselves in Newgate prison. Dunton even wrote their epitaph for them:

Men worse than goats
Who dress themselves in petticoats.

The Woman Hater's Lamentation, also of 1707, stated that over one hundred had been arrested for 'intriguing with one another'.

The hack journalist Ned Ward produced a sensational exposé of the molly houses in scandal-sheet terms with *A Complete and Humorous Account of the Remarkable Clubs and Societies in the Cities of London and Westminster* (1709). He revealed the presence of 'a particular gang of sodomitical wretches in this town who call themselves the Mollies' and who affect 'to speak, walk, tattle, curtsy, cry, scold' in the manner of 'lewd women'. They called each other 'sisters'. They talked about their 'husbands' and their children. According to Ward they went so far as to imitate pregnancy and birth, when one of them, dressed in nightgown and hood, was chosen 'to mimic the wry faces of a groaning woman' to be delivered of a wooden doll. After the ceremony they fell to their food and drink, provided by the tavern in which they met, and then engaged in 'filthy scandalous revels' and 'beastly obscenities'. How much is true, how much invention, is impossible to guess.

In the same year, however, a 'notorious gang of sodomites' was arrested in a brandy shop along Jermyn Street of which the owner was one of their number. Among them, also, was the foot-boy to the Duke of Ormonde. In London there emerged a pattern of activity. Even the boxes of the Theatre Royal, Drury Lane, were little 'nests' of male prostitutes and others.

*

Close encounters were not reserved for men. Certain female bagnios were open only to other women, such as Frances Bradshaw's establishment in Bow Street; rumours persisted of a rendezvous for female flagellants in Jermyn Street. The vogue for female players, inaugurated by the Restoration, included a fashion for apparently lesbian actresses. One familiar motif on the eighteenth-century stage was that of a woman, dressed as a man, who courts another woman. It was tantalising; it was sexy; it was loved by other women. Such scenes were often played on 'ladies' nights' when the audience was comprised of one sex only.

Female love was also one of the dominant motifs of the reign of Queen Anne, when a quarrel between two of her ladies became public knowledge. Sarah Jennings had known the queen since childhood; now she was Sarah Churchill, after her marriage to John Churchill, later to become Duke of Marlborough. In the course of sixteen years, before assuming the throne, Anne endured seventeen pregnancies of which twelve were stillborn and the rest died at an early age. The attentions of a male partner had almost destroyed her. No doubt these calamities intensified the bond between Anne and Sarah, already firmly planted in their mutual hatred of William III. But after she became monarch, Anne began to prefer a different lady.

Abigail Masham, her nurse and hairdresser, received signal tokens of the queen's favour. Sarah was incensed. She was a gossip and something of a termagant whose tirades rendered the queen more and more uncomfortable. Sarah's advisers and allies mounted an offensive against Abigail that took as its focus the question of queer sex. In one squib it is made explicit:

Her secretary she was not,
Because she could not write,

But had the conduct and care
Of some dark deeds at night.

It suggests the suspicion by which monarchs may be surrounded. Sarah wondered aloud how the queen could discourse among her women on the theme of reputation 'after having discovered so great a passion for such a woman, for sure there can be no great reputation in a thing so strange and unaccountable, to say no more of it?'

Anne was an invalid, with gout and related diseases, and can hardly be considered in the position of a sportive lover; but the succession of disastrous and painful pregnancies might justifiably explain her preference for female company. It had, in any case, become London news. One town hack, Arthur Maynwaring, wrote a pamphlet, *The Rival Duchess or the Court Incendiary* (1708), in which Abigail confesses to being 'rather addicted to another sort of passion, of having too great a regard for my own sex'. She is asked by a French lady of the court whether 'that female vice, which is the most detestable in nature, reigns among you, as it does with us in France?' She replies that 'we are arrived to as great perfection in sinning that way as you can pretend to'.

In the same year Delarivier Manley wrote a novel, *The New Atalantis*, in which she describes a cabal of lesbian lovers, alluding to 'rites' and to 'unaccountable intimacies' in which 'things may be strained a little too far'. Some couples go out to the theatres and public gardens in order to pick up female prostitutes and have sex with them. Other women dress as men. In case any reader missed the implications of this fantasy, a 'key' was appended in which the caballers were identified as ladies of the court. The novel may have been inaccurate and prurient but it met the expectations of the time.

A notice in the *Female Tatler* of September 1709 referred to 'the young lady in the parish of St Laurence, near Guildhall, that lately went to the coffee-house in man's clothes with the two 'prentices, called for a dish of Bohee [tea], smoked her pipe, and gave herself abundance of straddling masculine airs'.

A volume of 1718, Giles Jacob's *A Treatise of Hermaphrodites*, was principally comprised of female examples. But male ones could also be found. In *Epistle to Dr Arbuthnot* (1734) Alexander Pope descants upon Lord Hervey, an eighteenth-century courtier whose ambiguous persona excited comment.

> Now high, now low, now master up, now miss,
> And he himself one vile antithesis.
> Amphibious thing! that acting either part,
> The trifling head, or the corrupted heart!
> Fop at the toilet, flatt'rer at the board,
> Now trips a lady, and now struts a lord.

Lady Mary Wortley Montagu remarked that 'this world consists of men, women and Herveys'. Lord Hervey himself was the model for Miss Fanny in Henry Fielding's *Shamela* (1741). One of his political opponents, William Pulteney, addressed him as 'pretty sir' in a pamphlet and added that he 'was such a delicate hermaphrodite . . . you know that he is a lady himself; or at least such a nice composition of the two sexes, that it is difficult to distinguish which is more predominant'. Then he added an ambiguous observation. 'There is a certain, unnatural, reigning vice (indecent and almost shocking to mention) . . . it is well known that there must be two parties in this crime, the *pathic* and the *agent*; both equally guilty. I need not explain these any further.' Hervey immediately challenged Pulteney to a duel, from which they both escaped with only a scratch or two. But the damage had been done, and Hervey would ever after be associated with queerness.

Dildoes were now as fashionable as they were indispensable. A French traveller, Georges-Louis Lesage, noted in 1713 that certain women walked in St James's Park with baskets of dolls that attracted the attention of many young women. These dolls were in fact used to camouflage cylinders covered with cloth that were six inches long and one inch wide. This cylinder was celebrated in *Monsieur Thing's Origin* (1722):

> The engine does come up so near to nature,
> Can spout so pleasing, betwixt wind and water,
> Warm mild, or any other liquid softer,
> Slow as they please, or, if they please, much faster.

Theodora and Amaryllis, in *A Treatise of Hermaphrodites*, engage with one another until their strength ebbs; the woman on top 'withdrew and, taking another instrument in her hand, she used it on her companion with an injection of moisture which, with the rubbing, occasioned such a tickling, as to force a discharge of matter and facilitate the pleasure'. Jacob added that 'many lascivious females divert themselves one with another at this time in the city'.

Dildoes were inevitably associated with female masturbation. A much circulated treatise touches upon that theme. The anonymous *Onania; Or the Heinous Sin of Self-Pollution with all its Frightful Consequences* was published in the early eighteenth century. It is essentially pornography disguised as a moral treatise.

> I began, sir, the folly at eleven years of age; was taught it by my mother's chamber maid . . . we took all opportunities of committing it, and invented all the ways which were capable to heighten the titillation . . . We, in short, shamefully pleasured one another, as well as each ourselves . . . for above half year past I have had a swelling that thrust out from my body, as big and almost as hard and as long or longer than my thumb. Which inclined me to excessive lustful desires, and from it there issues a moisture or slipperiness to that degree that I am almost continually wet.

The dildoes might be made out of ivory or glass, or on occasion of India rubber, and came in all sizes; the glass vessels were often filled with a milky liquid that could be pumped out at an appropriate moment. Some were manipulated by hand while others were strapped on so that the woman could mimic the use of the male member; they were readily available, and one shop in Leicester Fields sold nothing else.

NEWGATE

12

Good golly Miss Molly

No real sense of privacy existed in eighteenth-century London; the private body easily became the public body. On a Sunday night in February 1726 a number of constables and law officers converged upon Mother Clap's in Field Lane, Holborn; the streets and exits were blocked and forty 'notorious sodomites' were hauled to Newgate. The unusually large raid seized the public imagination, with suggestions that the accused should be castrated in open court or that 'the hangman seal up his scrotum with a hot iron'. Three of them were literally strung up at Tyburn.

Mother Clap's was a molly house, its clientele known as mollies. Molly is already a familiar term in this history. The word may simply be a corruption of Mary, an old term of endearment, but it might be derived from the Latin for woman, *mulier*, or soft, *mollis*. In the eighth century Alcuin had written '*molles sunt effeminati*', mollies are effeminate males. The thirteenth-century patriarch, Theodore, used the word in the same sense. So it is deeply rooted.

The February raiders had been preceded by the agents of the Society for the Reformation of Manners who had come to spy and report. They must themselves have posed as queers in order to gain access. One of them, Samuel Stephens, testified that 'I have seen twenty or thirty of them together, kissing and hugging and making love (as they called it) in a very indecent manner. Then they used to go out by couples into another room and, when they came back, they would tell what they had been doing, which, in their dialect, they called marrying.' The room with a bed in it was known as 'the chapel'. They could be heard talking. 'Pray, sir – Dear sir – Lord, how can you serve me so – I swear I'll cry out – You're a wicked devil – And you've a bold face – Eh, you dear little Toad! Come buss.'

Mother Clap ran a coffee house; to procure liquor for her customers she went next door to the Bunch of Grapes, making a large profit on the transactions with her befuddled gentlemen. No doubt she also pimped for male prostitutes. In her defence she stated that 'I hope it will be considered that I am a woman, and therefore it cannot be thought that I would ever be concerned in such practices'. Nobody believed her. She was sentenced to two years in prison, and was consigned to the public pillory in Smithfield where she was treated so roughly that she twice fainted; she died in Newgate.

Before Mother Clap's was raided there had been some sensational or notorious trials. In 1721, at the Old Bailey, one young witness, Nicholas Leader, testified that George Duffus had embraced and kissed him, calling him 'my dear'. Duffus told him that he meant 'no harm, nothing but love'. Then he 'forcibly entered my body about an inch, as near as I can guess; but in struggling I threw him off once more, before he had made an emission, and having thus forced him to withdraw he emitted in his own hand and, clapping it on the tail of my shirt, said *Now you have it!*' The evidence may have saved Duffus from more severe punishment, since the charge of sodomy demanded proof that emission occurred during anal intercourse. Duffus himself was highly religious, and used to encounter his young men at the meeting houses of dissenters where he engaged in devout conversation before inviting them home. Another young man was snared in this manner, and admitted Duffus to bed when it was too late for him to return home. 'I readily consented, as I not at all suspecting his design; but we had not been long in bed before he began to kiss me and take hold of my privities. *How lean you be*, says he. *Do but feel how fat I am!*' Once again no 'spermatic injection', as it was called, could be proven and so Duffus escaped hanging and was consigned instead to prison and the pillory. The actual sperm or seed was believed to be the token of male identity, and was therefore too precious to be wasted or abused.

Other men were less subtle. John Dicks immobilised his potential partner with hot ale and gin at alehouses in Chancery Lane and Fetter Lane, close enough to carry the inebriated boy from one to the other. 'The prisoner unbuttoned my breeches,' the witness said, 'and turned me on my face, and tried to enter my body, but whether he did or not, I was not sensible enough to be certain.' The fact that the boy was not 'certain' may have saved Dicks from hanging.

Three constables were given a special warrant 'to apprehend sodomites'. They decided, after drinking at an alehouse in Moorfields, to try a little entrapment. One of them, Thomas Newton, took his position on a walk in Upper Moorfields by the side of a wall. 'So I takes a turn that way, and leans over the wall. In a little while the prisoner passes by, and looks hard at me, and at a small distance from me, stands up against the wall, as if he was going to make water.' Slowly the solitary man, William Brown, edged closer and closer to Newton until they were standing together. 'It is a very fine night,' Brown said. 'Ay,' Newton replied, 'and so it is.' The man guided Newton's hand to the bulge in his breeches, whereupon Newton grabbed hold of his penis and called out for the other two constables. When asked why he had taken 'indecent liberties', the prisoner gave a very interesting response. 'I did it because I thought I knew him, and I think there is no crime in making what use I please of my own body.' That was a libertarian sentiment which would not be heard again in public discourse for 250 years. How the man came to deliver this astonishing plea is not known.

His defence was not successful. A contemporary wrote that 'the other day, passing by Moorfields whilst Brown, the sodomite, stood in the pillory, I could not help making some reflections on the shower of rotten eggs, dead cats and turnip tops that the gentlemen of the mob were pleased to compliment him with on that occasion'.

It is not curious that witnesses to the act or acts could often be found. Sometimes they lived and slept in the same chamber, suggesting a degree of familiarity or unconcern. It was revealed that Charles Banner, accused of attempting sodomy on a boy of fifteen, kept a school in Smithfield. 'A school?' the judge asked. 'Does anybody trust their children with him?' It seemed that many did, and their testimony led to his acquittal.

At other times the witness could hear and see what was happening in the next room; it might have been no more than a slit in the partition, or small hole, or a crevice in the door, but it was enough to suggest that this was a far more public world. On one occasion a servant in a tavern off Drury Lane heard two men kissing one another in an upstairs chamber. With a colleague he took a ladder into the yard of the tavern and climbed it so that he could look into the chamber window; there he 'saw such actions as was very unseemly for men to offer'. The use of the ladder was ingenious. Another man, Thomas Doulton, was obliged to fill the pillory 'for endeavouring (to use the canting term) to discover the "windward passage" upon one Joseph Yates'.

The raid on Mother Clap's was followed by other raids on molly houses in the capital. Soon after, 'seven small-sized rogues were seized at a house of evil repute' in the notorious White Cross Place. They may have been children. It was said that 'God never made White Cross Place'. A gang 'of haunchmen, alias endorsers' was arrested in Westminster; an endorser, in legal terms, was one who made an entry on the back of something. In July Robert Whale and York Horner, otherwise known as Peggy and Pru, were arrested for keeping a molly house in King Street, Westminster. Mr Mugg, known as Aunt Mugg, was prosecuted for a molly house in Windmill Street.

Thomas Wright had managed a molly house in Christopher's Alley, Moorfields, before moving his establishment to Beech Lane. One secret agent reported that 'I went to the prisoner's house in Beech Lane, and there I found a company of men fiddling and dancing and singing bawdy songs, kissing and using their hands in a very unseemly manner . . . in a large room there we found one a-fiddling and eight more a-dancing country dances making vile motions and singing "Come, let us bugger finely". Then they sat in one another's laps, talked bawdy, and practiced a great many indecencies. There was a door in the great room, which opened into a little room, where there was a bed, and into this little room several of the company went.'

Molly houses might also be situated in the private rooms of taverns or alehouses. In Soho the Red Lion accommodated rooms at the back, as did brandy shops in Drury Lane. The Three Shoes in Moorfields and the Three Tobacco Rolls in Covent Garden had many molly customers. Clusters of similar venues could be found at Charing Cross, Moorfields and Smithfield. A 'club of pederasts' met at the Bunch of Grapes in Clare Market. The Royal Oak, at the corner of St James's

Square, was also well known; a neighbour testified that 'I have seen men in his back room behave themselves sodomitically, by exposing to each other's sight what they ought to have concealed. I have heard some of them say, "mine is the best, yours has been Battersea'd." I do not know what they meant by that expression.' 'Battersea'd' meant to be enamelled, after the enamel produced at York House, Battersea. It may have been some kind of preparation or mixture to deal with venereal infection.

Individuals were of course found beyond the setting of the molly houses. Churches were popular. Two men were caught with their trousers down in the porch of the parish church at Stepney one night, and the subsequent jury concluded that 'they were no better than two of those degenerated miscreants from the race of men called sodomites'.

One of the tour guides for St Paul's Cathedral in 1730 heard noises in the great church. 'I looked through the light of the Newel Stairs,' he reported and 'discovered [two men] in a very indecent posture.' He added that 'Huggins was stooping very low, so that I could not see his head, his breeches were down, his shirt was turned upon his back, and his backside was bare. Holliwell was standing close by, with his fore parts to the other's posteriors, and his body was in motion.' The guide locked them in a side aisle and ran for the clerk of the works and the dean. Huggins and Holliwell were eventually taken away and met with the familiar penalty of the pillory, soon after which they both died from their injuries.

The cathedral was more than a monument. It was a convenience. At a later date two men were found having sex in the courtyard behind the chapter house. They were surprised by a constable, with the name of Obert Pert, who called out 'in the name of God, what are you doing? Who or what are you?' One of the two men, Blair, said that he went to the place 'to ease Nature'.

'It is in a very odd way,' the constable replied.

Blair lost his composure. 'Damn you, sir, if I must tell you, I was at shite.'

The other man, Deacon, testified that he had gone to piss. He said to the constable that he was doing 'no ill'.

'What,' Pert answered, 'you are two buggerers I suppose?'

Deacon gave an odd reply. 'There is no such thing.'

Both men were found guilty as charged.

Churches and churchyards were fully employed for furtive sexual encounters, perhaps with some folk memory of the uses of churches for sanctuary. Another favoured spot was the area, close to St Clement Dane's, where Fleet Street and the Strand meet. Thieving Lane by Westminster Abbey and the immediate neighbourhood of the church of St Giles in the Fields were other ports of call. A clergyman complained from the pulpit of St Dunstan's, Fleet Street, that his church was used by males 'who wanted but convenience to perpetrate the most detestable of crimes'.

A molly house by Newgate and the Old Bailey, not far from St Paul's, arranged a ball where a witness reported men 'calling one another "my dear" and hugging, kissing and tickling one another . . . assuming effeminate voices and airs, some telling others that they ought to be whipped for not coming to school more frequently'. These gay balls were never decorous. One masquerader threw a box of snuff on the back of another's dress to give the impression that he was 'offensively besmeared' with shit. In 1728 nine men were arrested at a house in Black Lion Yard, Whitechapel, belonging to Jonathan Muff, known as Miss Muff, and taken to Newgate or Bridewell. At the subsequent trials of these and other mollies, the slang of the streets surfaces once more. One man accosted a foot soldier in St James's Park and offered to provide him with 'a green gown upon the grass', or to have sex with him in the open air. One drummer boy, Rowley Hanson, 'became as common as the night'. The police were informed that a group of sodomites had their 'tail quarters' in an empty house off Marylebone.

Similar actions were reported at the trials – thrusting hands into another man's breeches, feeling his private parts, sticking his own penis into another's hand, forcible kissing with his tongue, wriggling in his lap for the purpose of causing ejaculation. The size of the penis was a subject of speculation in the courtroom. John Marten's *Gonosologium Novum* (1707) contained the information that 'in short men it is generally observed to be longer than in tall men. In half-witted people it is generally pretty large, the length of the largest being commonly, when erected, nine inches long and four inches in circumference.' Marten would have known. He was a surgeon.

In the same period Charles Hitchen was the under-marshal of the City, responsible for policing part of the capital. He was an active member of the Society for the Reformation of Manners and had to keep an eye on mollies; but he himself was queer. He had as his assistant Jonathan Wild who became notorious as the 'thief-taker general', engaged in fencing stolen goods. So Hitchen was part of a murky world where the unruly ruled. It is not surprising that he took bribes from the managers of molly houses to avert their prosecution. Hitchen had a fancy for the group of mollies near the Old Bailey and took Wild to their 'house'. He told Wild that he was about to meet 'a company of he-whores'. Wild asked if they were 'hermaphrodites'. 'No, you fool, they are sodomites, such as deal with their sex instead of females.'

On arriving at the molly house Hitchen was addressed as 'madam' and 'your ladyship'; he 'dallied with the young sparks', but the dalliance came to an abrupt end when a party of gentlemen, no doubt with ready money, entered. Hitchen was abandoned by the mollies for more savoury meat. He was mortified, and threatened revenge on the whole pack of them. He took exception to the fact that the young mollies rejected his advances, and so he set a trap. As they came back from a ball in Holborn, he arrested them in all their finery. They were dressed as milkmaids, shepherdesses, or ladies of fashion with hoops and petticoats; their faces were liberally decorated with plaster, patches and paint. Once taken, they were paraded through the streets of London before being dispatched to the workhouse; one of their number, however, threatened to provide evidence against Hitchen himself, and the charges against the mollies were dropped by the lord mayor.

Yet the fall of Hitchen came soon after. In the spring of 1727 he took a young man, Richard Williamson, to bed at the Talbot Inn, where he was a well-known customer. He would often bring a soldier to the inn, and disappear with him into a private apartment. But Richard Williamson was not a willing partner; he told the incident to a relative, and together they concealed themselves behind a door until through a keyhole they spied Hitchen *in flagrante* with another young man.

When he was eventually led to the pillory, his friends and colleagues put up a screen of carts and carriages to prevent him from being attacked by the mob, and a great battle ensued. After half an hour Hitchen himself was so severely beaten that he was taken down. Consigned to Newgate for the next six months, he was stripped of his office as under-marshal. He died soon after. It is a case of the biter bit, or the molly-taker mollied, but it is also an interesting example of the ways in which the criminal underworld and sexual underworld met in eighteenth-century London. They were all essentially outcasts.

James Dalton was a street thug of the familiar type, part pickpocket and part highway robber. In his gang were two professional blackmailers who specialised in 'putting the bite' on London queers. It was also known as 'the common bounce'. John Mitchell, alias Nurse Mitchell, sat down on a bench in St James's Park and told the man beside him that 'he could show nine inches' and asked him whether he could do the same. The victim made his excuses and left. But Mitchell followed him and said that 'if he did not give him a guinea he would swear sodomy to him'. Mitchell was eventually charged with extortion. Another of Dalton's associates, James Oviat, or Miss Kitten, also pursued an unfortunate gentleman for money, 'saying, if he would not give it to him, he would swear sodomy against him'. The records only report the blackmailers who failed. Any number of them may have been able to apply pressure to unsuspecting victims. Some of those unfairly accused might have seemed effeminate, so that their defences were already down, and others may have been so nervous that in the phrase of the time they were 'known to pay' simply to avoid controversy and confrontation. Others may just have been in the wrong place at the wrong time of day. This is a world of bullying, intimidation and terror about which nothing is really known. We can only suspect that it was an intrinsic part of the queer world of London. The moral seemed to be that it was wise to avoid parks or other well-known rendezvous.

Mollies were not at all like the fops or beaux on the stage. They were from the lower classes, typically manual workers or labourers who liked to become women. James Stevens was a waterman on the Thames, a strenuous occupation, but his neighbours testified that he caused a commotion 'by going about in women's apparel in a very impudent and insolent manner, insulting the neighbourhood'; he may not have been a molly at all, but a compulsive cross-dresser. One of those arrested was a milk-man and another a wool-comber. Theirs was of course a parody of the female, rather like the 'drag' acts of more recent periods. Nor were they anything like the pretty boys who 'knew nothing and did everything'. They were rough, and their language was not choice.

They were called by various names, among them Miss Betty or Miss Nancy, Plump Nelly or Primrose Mary. In certain notorious trials of 1726 some were named as Garter Mary, 'a man who sells garters about the streets', Fish Hannah, a fish-monger, Mary Magdalen, Mademoiselle Gent or Orange Dib together with various other Misses and Mademoiselles. Aunt England was a soap-boiler, and Aunt May an upholsterer. Lucy Cooper was a strapping coal-heaver and Kitty Cambric was a coal merchant. Some had puzzling names, including Susan Guzzle and Johannah the Ox-Cheek Woman. They screamed familiar insults at each other. 'Oh, you bold pullet, I'll break all your eggs!' or 'Oh, I will beat the milk out of your breasts, I will so!' or 'Where have you been, you saucy queen?' They called each other 'she' or 'her'. Many of them were for some reason called 'Sukey'. Anal sex was known as 'the pleasant deed', while the active partner was said 'to do the story'.

John Cowper, aka the Princess Seraphina, was described as a 'mollycull', one of those 'runners that carried messages between gentlemen . . . going of sodomitical errands'. At Cowper's trial, Mary Poplet, landlady of the Two Sugar Loaves, was called to testify. 'I have known her Highness a pretty while . . . she commonly used to wear a white gown and a scarlet cloak with her hair frizzled and curled all around her forehead; and then she would so flutter her fan and make such fine curtsies that you would not have known her from a woman: she takes great delight in balls and masquerades.' Cowper was a butcher by trade. Butchers and bakers, orange-sellers and barbers were an integral part of the fraternity or, rather, sisterhood. Many molly establishments may have been family concerns. One eighteen-year-old servant and male whore told a client, 'I suppose I am not handsome enough for you but, if you don't like me, I have got a pretty younger brother.' Some young men aspiring to the trade would wear trousers with tears or holes in them to advertise their availability.

One of the peculiarities of the molly was the aspiration to fake grandeur like that of Princess Seraphina. John Hyons liked to be known as Queen Iron; he also called himself, or was called, Pippin Mary. Lady Godiva was a waiter, and the Duchess of Gloucester another butcher. It was innocent enough, and sufficiently diverting to keep the men amused. But the mollies were on the periphery of a dangerous world. In the subsequent trials there is much evidence of violent quarrels and vicious arguments; it was difficult to know whom to trust, and one of their number was denounced as 'a treacherous . . . blowing-up mollying bitch'.

Four trials, in particular, captured public attention. Richard Branson was accused of importuning James Fasset, a sixteen-year-old. Fasset testified that Branson 'asked me if I never got any girls, or if I never fucked them'. The boy said that he had no such thoughts. Branson then kissed him and sucked his lips. He asked another question. Had the boy ever frigged himself? No. Branson said that 'if I would go back, he would learn me'. All this time the boy kept a tight hold of his breeches. 'He asked me if I had my maidenhead . . . If I had he should be very glad to take it from me, but supposed I saved it for a young woman.'

Michael Levi lived in Holborn and possessed a stall beside an alehouse, the Baptist's Head. One night he asked Benjamin

Taylor, twelve years old, to take up some of his boxes to the room which he rented in the alehouse itself. Once there Levi locked the door, flung the boy on the bed and proceeded to rape him. Then two other boys came forward, one of them saying that 'he thought the prisoner had pissed on him'. He was likely to have confused semen with urine.

Isaac Broderick was a schoolmaster at a school run by the Company of Coopers who had taken a liking to some of his pupils. Eventually it came out. One of the young boys, Edward Calley, aged ten, told his grandfather that 'his master had served him as the two men had served one another that stood in the pillory'. He was a knowing London youth.

John Holloway met Henry Wolf in the street, and asked him for directions. This seems to be a typical scenario, suggesting that 'asking for directions' was more than what it seemed. A Londoner would surely know the way. But Holloway may have got more than he expected. Wolf put his arm about his waist, tickled him and took him to a local alehouse where he groped him. He then took the boy onto the streets and purchased for him a pint of wine, a nosegay and a penny custard. They were just passing Bedlam when Wolf suggested that they pay a visit to the mad people. Once there, they went into the necessary house (otherwise known as the bog house or house of office) where Holloway fellated him. Other such cases could be cited but it has become clear enough that the queer life of London could be difficult and hazardous. When one man was caught after the act he cried out 'My dear! My dear! First time! First time!'

Another dramatic episode occurred at the Mermaid Inn in Great Carter Lane. The landlady, Sarah Holland, testified that two customers, Richard Manning and John Davis, had taken a room on New Year's Eve 1744. She suspected something between them and had given them a chamber next to her own bedroom. She went over to a small glass partition between the two rooms and found them 'sitting facing one another with their knees jammed together'. She then observed them putting their hands into each other's breeches. They went over to the partition, as if to see 'the shade of any body' but she drew back and could not be detected. They carried on with their kissing and fondling.

Then Sarah rushed up to another lodger. 'I have heard talk of sodomites, and believe there are some here!' 'God forbid!' he replied. Another lodger had been called into her bedroom. 'I don't like the thoughts of them,' he said. But he also looked through the glass partition and saw them 'bussing' or kissing. The cry went up. Sarah called out 'You damned dogs! What are you doing of! Nasty fellows! Vile rogues!' One of the men eventually arrested, Richard Manning, was said to resemble 'an old rat in an iron cage' and 'did not make any attempt to go away'.

They were sentenced to be well whipped and Manning, at least, was consigned to prison. In his own defence John Davis testified that he was too drunk to know where he was or what he was doing. The jury did not believe him. But it must have occurred to some that the act of Sodom might appeal to any man who was drunk enough to ignore the possible consequences. It did not represent some particular temperament. It was a weakness common to men and women alike. Manning was walking along Fleet Street, just after his release from prison, when an acquaintance came up to him. 'So, Molly!' he said. Manning reacted in shock. 'I never mollied you!' Yet once again he was taken up by the constables.

Some convicted of sodomy were married men with children. This would cause no considerable surprise at a later date, but at this time it was widely believed that a married man, who had sired offspring, could not have committed the unmentionable sin. The wives and children were sometimes brought into court to confront the man's accusers. One caught in the act was a waterman who was father to several children. Another found guilty had been married for twenty-five years and had twelve children. A certain leniency of punishment was then in order. But not all were so lucky. An upholsterer of forty-three, with two children, was sentenced to death and at his execution stated that 'he hoped the world would not be so unjust as to upbraid his poor children with his unfortunate death'.

The punishment varied with the circumstance, the occasion and the magistrate. Some men faced the pillory and the prison, while for others the penalty was death. Some of them formed gangs to fight back against officers come to arrest them. They could be mean and violent as well as gay and effeminate. Some of them certainly became prostitutes, or pimps, or blackmailers; they might also be informers. Some of them, at least, were part of dirty and violent London.

The Life and Adventures of a FEMALE SOLDIER.

HANNAH SNELL, was born in *Fryer-Street* in the Parish of St. *Hellen's*, in the city of *Worcester*, in *England*, on the

13

Flats

'Two Kissing Girls of Spitalfields' were the subject of a ballad in 1728.

> She kisses all, but Jenny is her dear,
> She feels her bubbies, and she bites her ear:
> They to the garret or the cellar sneak,
> Play tricks, and put each other to the squeak.

Curiously enough such behaviour would probably have gone unnoticed or unmentioned in an earlier period. In another production of 1728, *Plain Reasons for the Growth of Sodomy*, the anonymous author declared that 'when I see two ladies kissing and slopping each other in a lascivious manner, and frequently repeating it, I am shocked to the last degree'.

Mother Courage ran a house exclusively for females in Suffolk Street while one in Bow Street catered for a similar clientele. Miss Redshawe held 'an extremely secretive discreet house of intrigue in Tavistock Street catering for ladies in the highest keeping'. Some wealthy married ladies also called there for furtive pleasures. It was widely believed that pregnant women were subject to unnatural lusts which might incline them towards their own sex.

In Harris's *List of Covent Garden Ladies*, a useful guide to the prostitutes of the town, published annually from 1757 to 1795, reference is made to Miss Wilson of Green Street,

Cavendish Square, whose burly physique was 'more calculated for the milk carrier than the soft delights of love'. Some women might then have become interested. The entry added that Miss Wilson had declared that 'a female bed-fellow can give more real joys than ever she experienced with the male part of the sex' and revealed that 'many of the pranks she has played with her own sex in bed (where she is as lascivious as a goat) have come to our knowledge'. One of those pranks might well have been the queer game of 'flats', involving the rubbing of female pudenda one against another. At the end of the seventeenth century it was described as a 'new game, called flats with a swinging clitoris'. At a later date it was known as a 'flat fuck'.

In 1730 Mary East married a young female friend under the name of James How; they moved to Poplar, in east London, where they kept an alehouse or inn for the next thirty-six years. James How also became a parish officer and fulfilled the duties without provoking comment. No one seemed to notice that in fact one woman was living in masquerade with another. The matter only came to light when a previous neighbour recognised How and proceeded to blackmail her. It was reported in the *Gentleman's Magazine* of July 1776 that in her female character How 'appeared to be a sensible well-bred woman, though in her male character she had always affected the plain plodding alehouse-keeper'. So she was a competent actor as well as a convincing cross-dresser. It was said that both women had been 'crossed in love' when they were young and had wished to avoid further disappointment. This was often given as the reason for female transvestism; it preserved male pride while palliating the female transgression.

In fact cross-dressing with or without queer connotations may not have been uncommon. It was a way of making a living in a predominantly male world where, as another girl who passed as a boy put it, 'boys could shift better for themselves than girls'; it invited respect where the union of two women might not; it was a way of avoiding unwanted male attention; it was a ready form of companionship, even if no sexual bond existed. It seems likely, too, that some people must have suspected the truth but were unwilling to voice it. How might have been eccentric and nothing more. She might have been jilted by a man, and to have taken her revenge in this way. She might have been too ugly to be accepted as a female. These were the contemporary explanations. It was always easier for a women to dress as a man than a man to dress as a woman. Sexual intercourse, of whatever description, was considered to be intrinsically less serious between females than between males; women had no fertile seed, according to contemporaneous medical texts, and therefore no waste of life was implied. There was also no fear of an unwanted pregnancy.

The roll call of honorary soldiers and sailors includes the names of Hannah Snell, Mary Anne Talbot, Mary Knowles and Christina Davies. All of them joined the army or the navy; they may have wanted the excitement of combat, but popular legend was that they had enlisted in order to keep company with serving husbands or lovers or to search for them. It was almost a plausible excuse. But a moment's acquaintance with female pirates, such as Ann Bonny and Mary Read, suggests that females could indeed be just as brave and ferocious as the males. They must have been good sailors and soldiers to survive for so long.

Hannah Snell joined the marines, and was injured in action. On her return to England she earned her living by appearing in full uniform in various minor theatres where she marched and sang. In her early years Christina Davies, according to a contemporary pamphlet, 'felt a love for boyish amusements and the pleasure she took in manly occupations'. She married; but her husband disappeared and she subsequently enlisted into the army under the name of Christopher Welsh. Eventually she opened a pub in the London docks called the Widow in Masquerade. She received a pension from the Royal Hospital of Chelsea for wounds received at the siege of Pondicherry in 1778, but her title as 'the Chelsea Amazon' was shared with Catherine Walsh who served with the Royal North British Dragoons or Scots Greys and was wounded in action during the Battle of Ramillies in 1706.

Mary Anne Talbot was better known as James Talbot, sailor. She ran the gamut of juvenile naval occupations as drummer, powder monkey, cabin boy and steward. She may have had queer longings because 'she actually made a conquest of the captain's niece . . . the young lady even went so far as to propose marriage'. On her return to England she was 'still inclined to masculine propensities'. She did now dress as a female 'though at times I could not so far forget my sea-faring habits, but frequently dressed myself and took excursions as a sailor'.

Some women dressed and acted as men simply in order to marry for money. Sarah Getson became John for an advantageous union, while another female was charged with marrying three different women. Sums of money sometimes exchanged hands, but often these counterfeit husbands stole the money and ran off. Nevertheless innocents were abroad. John Chivy was the perfect spouse and was married to the same woman for almost twenty years; only on his deathbed in 1764 was he pronounced to be female. In 1760 Samuel Bundy was discovered to be a female and was briefly jailed in Southwark 'for defrauding a young woman of money and apparel by marrying her'. But Mrs Bundy came forward to defend her supposed husband and refused to press charges. The *London*

Chronicle reported that 'there seems a strong love or friendship . . . as she keeps the prisoner company in her confinement'. Samuel Bundy was ordered to burn her female clothes, but that was the only punishment.

At the end of 1734 a Soho clergyman refused to sign a marriage certificate for John Mountford, tailor, and Mary Cooper, spinster; he noted that he 'suspected two women, no certificate'. Two other London females were more fortunate in 1737, when the clergyman wrote briefly that 'by the opinion after matrimony my clerk judged they were both women, if the person by name John Smith be a man, he's a little short fair thin man not above five foot. After marriage I almost could prove them both women, the one was dressed as a man [with] thin pale face and wrinkled chin.' Yet he still joined them in matrimony. A note of 1 October 1747 recorded the marriage of John Ferren and Deborah Nolan to the effect that 'the supposed John Ferren was discovered, after the ceremony were over, to be in person a woman'. It seems that no further action was taken. Many poor clergymen could be found in Fleet Street and its environs ready to marry anyone and everyone for a fee. Barbara Hill had taken the name of John Brown before marrying another woman 'with whom she has lived very agreeably since'; John Brown had previously worked as a stonecutter's apprentice and a London post-chaise driver. There may have been an indeterminate boundary between young beardless men and young women. Their Shakespearean heroes or heroines might have included Viola, Portia and Rosalind.

Henry Fielding took up the strange life of Mary Hamilton in *The Female Husband*, a pamphlet of 1746. She had been arrested in the autumn of that year for posing as a male physician by the name of Charles Hamilton. His wife, Mary Price, was supposed to have testified in court that 'after marriage they had lain together several nights and that the said pretended Charles Hamilton who had married her aforesaid entered her body several times, which made this woman believe at first that the said Hamilton was a real man'. It was believed that Mary Hamilton had deployed a leather dildo, although it is not clear how this instrument had deceived the new wife. It may have occurred to some that Mary Price actually enjoyed the experience.

Hamilton's queerness was no crime, but for the charge of vagrancy and of 'imposing on His Majesty's subjects' it was declared that 'we, the Court, do sentence her or him' to four public whippings and six months' hard labour. It was a harsh punishment and may have caught Henry Fielding's eye. It was subsequently discovered that she had married anywhere between three and fourteen women over a period of years, and out of this Fielding created a narrative that is essentially fiction with a stratum of fact somewhere within it. This is of course true of most eighteenth-century accounts of sexual transgression. It was the transgression, and not the sex, that enraged the crowds who watched her pass them on the way to court. She had belittled the sanctity of marriage and had breached the laws of social custom. That was why she was punished. She had become literally and legally a vagrant, inconstant and unsettled.

The custom of female queerness was so common, and so universally understood, that in the spring of 1749 the *London Evening Post* advertised '*The Sappho-an*. An heroic poem of three cantos, in the Ovidian style, describing the pleasures which the fair sex enjoy with each other.' In his pornographic *An Essay on Woman*, John Wilkes mentions that 'there is a bastard plant called clitoris, much of the same nature, although seldom large . . . The Lesbian ladies knew perfectly the virtues of it.'

Even Swift's Gulliver mentions it: 'I expected every moment that my master would accuse the Yahoos of those unnatural appetites in both sexes, so common among us.' This was no longer the secret, or the silent, activity. It was rumoured that notable lesbians were invited to join the Hellfire Club, at Medmenham Abbey by the Thames, where they could freely enjoy their sport in various orgies and rituals. Such habits were reported to be rife in female boarding schools, in servants' quarters, and in the female sections of workhouses where 'grubbling' or groping in the dark was common.

Charlotte Charke was another female in disguise. At the age of seventeen she took to the stage, where she specialised in 'breeches parts' or male characters; they seemed to suit her and she began wearing male apparel off the stage as well and assumed the name of Charles Brown. She became a sausage-maker, a playwright, a pastry cook, a farmer, a strolling player, a waiter, a puppet-master, a gentleman's valet and the proprietor of the Charlotte Charke Tavern on Drury Lane. She also wrote *A Narrative of the Life of Mrs Charlotte Charke* (1755) in which she recorded 'mad pranks' as well as her adoption of male habits including 'a shrug of the shoulders and a scratch of the head, with a hasty demand for small beer'. She seems to have been a born actor, a Proteus of trades and personalities, and she was also twice married with a daughter. She may have been *en travesti* but it is not clear that she had queer relations with other women. She never admitted as much but, at the end of her *Narrative*, she confesses that 'I have, throughout the whole course of my life, acted in contradiction to all points of regularity . . . There is none in the world *more fit than myself to be laughed at*.' But her ability to dress and behave as a man does suggest the precariousness of conventional sexual roles with consequent social unease. That is why some unlucky women, caught at the wrong time or in the wrong place, were whipped for it.

By the 1770s, at the latest, queer women were often called 'tommies'. It was the female equivalent of 'molly'. It is mentioned in *The Adulteress* (1773) that 'Unnatural crimes like these my satire vex / I know a thousand *Tommies* amongst the sex'. And in 1777 the anonymous author of *A Sappick Epistle* noted of Sappho herself that 'she was the first Tommy the world has upon record; but to do her justice, though there have been many Tommies since, yet we have never had but one Sappho'.

Another female who mounted the stage in male clothes was Margaret or Peg Woffington who also specialised in breeches parts. She was a well-known 'beauty' whose charms appealed to both sexes equally, as a contemporary squib makes clear:

> That excellent Peg
> Who showed such a leg,
> When lately she dressed in men's clothes.
> A creature uncommon
> Who's both man and woman
> And chief of the belles and the beaux.

She was the only woman member of the Beefsteak Club, which included Garrick and Hogarth, and eventually became its president. The interest in female actors playing male parts had subsided by the end of the eighteenth century, but was revived at a later date in Victorian music-hall acts. It might be suggested that the breeches parts became unfashionable precisely at the time when the public consciousness of lesbianism reached a high level, but the connection cannot be proven.

In 1746 a prostitute, Ann Ellingworth, persuaded a man and wife to join her for a pot of ale in the Castle at Seven Dials.

At her subsequent trial for robbing the husband, Ann testified that Mrs King had attempted to seduce her. She declared that 'Terence King's wife went to put her hands up my petticoats and I did not like it from a woman's hands. I had never known such doings from our own sex . . . Mrs King and I had some words. As I stood at the door she clapp'd her hands up my coats: I said I was never used so by a woman, I don't know what you mean by it! And with that the husband went to strike me.' The jury believed Ann's account, and she was acquitted. It was perhaps not very unusual for one woman to proposition another.

Hester Thrale, the quondam companion and confidante of Samuel Johnson, was beady-eyed on the subject of queer women and monitored what was for her an increasingly gruesome situation from the 1770s to 1793. From Turkey to Twickenham the signs could be found, the latter area in particular being known for its accomplished sapphists. Here, for example, lived Lady Mary Wortley Montagu whose travels in Turkey, and sojourns among Turkish women, led her into curious and unfamiliar habits. It was said that she had established her own harem of young women.

Thrale noted with an early entry in her diary that 'this horrible vice has a Greek name now and is called Sapphism . . . it is now grown common to suspect impossibilities (such I think them) whenever two ladies live too much together'. She mentioned that 'that house of Miss Rathbone's is now supposed to have been but a cage of unclean birds, living in a sinful celibàt. Mercy on us!' The danger came ever closer. The actress Mrs Siddons even warned Mrs Thrale that her 'sister was in personal danger once from a female friend of this sort'. It was everywhere, and Hester Thrale fell into a moral panic. 'Why was Miss Weston so averse to any marriage I am thinking . . .

Colonel Barry had a good escape of Miss Trefusis if all be true.' Nobody was safe from the tommy. Thrale was also on the alert for queer males whom she called 'finger twirlers'. One was known as 'the It' for his exotic ways. London had become a 'sink' for all sins, and she lamented the frequency of that 'unnatural vice among men (now so modish)'.

A German traveller, Johann von Archenholz, published a book of his travels in 1787 in which he commented that in London 'there are females who avoid all intimate intercourse with the opposite sex, confining themselves to their own sex. These females are called lesbians. They have small societies, known as Anandrinic Societies, of which Mrs Y, formerly a famous London actress, was one of the presidents.' Mrs Y was Mary Anne Yates, a tragedy actress at the Drury Lane theatre, about whom strange rumours circulated. She was considered to be stately, haughty and hard.

More news was published in December 1792. The *Bon Ton Magazine* disclosed the presence in London of a female whipping club that met on Thursday evening in Jermyn Street. It was comprised of 'female flagellists' who had 'grown weary of wedlock in all its accustomed forms' and wanted to add spice to their encounters with one another; they wished also 'to keep their propensities, for such we may fairly call them, profoundly secret'. They were not altogether secret, however, because the correspondent of *Bon Ton* remarked that they choose their positions, stooping down or standing up, by lot. The chairwoman of the little gathering began the session with a lecture and then a practical demonstration; it was she who decided whether the 'engine of duty' should be applied to the thighs, the buttocks or the 'cave of Cupid'. It sounds remarkably like a male fantasy, as exemplified in the semi-pornographic novellas of the period, but the fact that it could be conceived at all is an indication of the sexual possibilities of the city. What could be imagined could also be performed.

One of the most famous female queers of the late eighteenth century was Anne Damer. She was considered to be 'singular' – 'she wears a man's hat and shoes – and a jacket also like a man's – as she walks about the fields with a hooking stick'. Hester Thrale, ever on the watch for 'singularity', noted in her diary of 17 June 1790: 'Mrs Damer, a lady much suspected to liking her own sex in a criminal way.' It was considered to be 'a joke in London now to say such a one visits Mrs Damer'. She was partial to actresses or perhaps actresses were partial to her.

Female marriages were still part of the early-nineteenth-century world. In 1827, Mary Shelley assisted Mary Diana Dods to elope to Paris with her lover, Isabella Robinson. Dods eventually took the name of Walter Sholto Douglas, who just happened to be the husband of Isabella Robinson. Under another assumed name, David Lyndsay, she wrote books and articles; the only biography of her, by Betty T. Bennett, is entitled *Mary Diana Dods: A Gentleman and a Scholar*. Another interesting example came to light in the *Edinburgh Annual Register* of 1815 when a black woman of twenty successfully posed as the captain on the foretop of a ship. She then came to London as a prizefighter, for which she gained great plaudits, and it was reported that 'in her manner she exhibits all the traits of a British tar, and takes her grog with her late messmates with the greatest gaiety . . . She declared her intention of again entering the service as a volunteer.'

14

Tiddy dolls

Mr Fribble has emerged in an earlier chapter as the model of a mid-eighteenth-century queer. He was the creation of David Garrick who introduced him to the stage in a farce of 1747, *Miss in Her Teens*. 'We drink tea, hear the chat of the day, invent fashions for the ladies, make models of 'em, and cut out patterns in paper.' If eventually Mr Fribble should marry 'the domestic business will be taken off her hands; I shall make the tea, comb the dogs, and dress the children myself . . . But my dear *creature*, who put on your cap to-day? They have made a fright of you, and it's as yellow as old Lady Crowfoot's neck . . . What shall I do? I shall certainly catch my death! Where's my cambric handkerchief, and my salts? I shall certainly have my hysterics!'

In the same year Nathaniel Lancaster's *The Pretty Gentleman* asked the reader to 'observe that fine complexion! Examine that smooth, that velvety skin! View this pallor which spreads itself over his countenance. Hark, with what a feminine softness his accents steal their way through his half-opened lips!' He might be known as a fribble or a whiffle, a jemmy or a macaroni, with names such as Lord Dimple and Marjorie Pattypan.

Waterloo Sedley, in Thackeray's *Vanity Fair* (1848), announced himself with the words 'I am a dressy man'. It was remarked that 'though rather uneasy if the ladies looked at him . . . and though he blushed and turned away alarmed at their glances, it was chiefly from dread lest they should make love to him'. Yet when posted to Calcutta 'he gave the best bachelor dinners'.

The effeminate male has been parodied or satirised for the best part of a thousand years and continues in the pantomime dames of the day before yesterday. This in turn leads to the question at the heart of this book. What is the connection between queerness and the city? It is not confined to the city, but it is identified with it. It is no accident that the two great urban centres of classical antiquity, Athens and Rome, were well known for their homosexual ambience.

The atmosphere of London, too, floats over the familiar claims of the family and of traditional loyalties; London is by its nature subversive, suborning previously tight bonds. That is why it symbolised abstract space and abstract justice instead of the claims of kinship. Other forms of community emerged, entirely estranged from the family or blood kinship. These were the communities formed by those of similar tastes and habits; they could be part of the culture of the streets or of the taverns, or they might be communities of strangers associated with a certain public footpath or bog house. Some of them were the anonymous wanderers of London, linked briefly by furtive sex in a dark corner. Some of them claimed the city night as their own. The city was the home and haven of anonymity.

Queer men and women were able in the multifarious city to adopt different personae, with changes of dress and behaviour, being a serious citizen at one time and a screaming molly at another. The women could change into men's clothes in a moment and disport themselves in the tavern or the coffee shop. In a society which relied upon ostensible gradations of rank and dress, the rule-benders of eighteenth-century London had a distinct advantage. They could be anyone.

Urban types, as popularised by the essayists and playwrights, might also be the pillars of the gay world; the confirmed bachelor, the actor, the theatregoer, the dandy or macaroni, the milliner and the delivery boy, all were ambiguous. They had only to play to stereotype to be an intrinsic part of London.

The crowds, the spaces, the alleys, the incomprehensible babble of voices, induced in some a creeping sense of chaos and confusion where all boundaries were ignored. The crowd itself could be a sexual experience. You could see, and be seen by, many others, with the delight of the gaze or the shared look. Anyone might become available. The queer could enter the markets or the assembly rooms, the taverns or the bog houses, and observe the restless waves of Londoners bent upon excitement and the unexpected. The city was known to be both a jungle and a labyrinth where gay life could flourish, each street leading to another and then another; there was no end to the possibilities or to the adventures. It provoked the restless need to explore.

As Italo Calvino put it in *Invisible Cities*, 'cities, like dreams, are made up of desires and fears, even if the thread of their discourse is secret, their rules are absurd, their perspective deceitful, and everything conceals something else'. The city was a phantasmagoria or a dreamscape, therefore, upon which the queer man or woman could project the most illicit longings. It was the most open and public place but also the most private and furtive space.

The migrants who moved to London were entering a world entirely different from anything they had known before. Even if it could be deadly it was undoubtedly exciting. Sexual experimentation, and sexual excess, were thereby encouraged. The new sense of anonymity also warmed the atmosphere; here were men and women packed together, practically living in each other's chambers. The city sexualised everything and everybody within its ambit. That is why the masquerades and the pleasure gardens, the tavern grounds and the bagnios were hives of illicit activity.

In London was situated the largest sexual market in the country, rivalling the meat market of Smithfield. In London we can locate the various prostitutes of both sexes – the soldiers who acted as hustlers in St James's Park and elsewhere, the young boys who had been trained in service, the effeminate men, the men dressed as women, the women dressed as men, the street boys who congregated at certain corners or by certain public monuments, the inhabitants of brothels who rarely saw the light of day, all of these were part of London trade. More rich men lived in London than in any other part of England; the city therefore acted as a powerful draw to those who wished to earn their living in a certain way. Great clerics and great courtiers had their houses or palaces in the city. It was perhaps not entirely foolish of the London crowd of the sixteenth century, for example, to conclude that sodomy was the particular vice of 'the church and the court'.

The city was also a great stage upon which men and women saw themselves. It offered the arena for theatrical self-definition and the proclamation of difference. Some were applauded, and others condemned, according to the taste of the moment. But in a sense the city itself seemed to shape their sexuality; it may have emboldened and inspired them to create a new identity at the same time as they struggled with the novel complexities of their lives.

Being queer almost became the fashion of the mid eighteenth century. In 1746 Charles Churchill wrote: 'Go where we will at every time and place, / Sodom confronts, and stares us in the face.'

Tobias Smollett caricatured the queer man in *Roderick Random* (1748). Captain Whiffle of the Royal Navy had flowing long hair 'in ringlets, tied behind with a ribbon'; he wore a white hat topped by a feather, a pink silk coat, a white satin waistcoat embroidered with gold while his 'crimson velvet breeches scarcely descended so low as to meet his silk stockings'. Life in the forces was not necessarily kind for the sodomite. One soldier earned five hundred lashes for the act in 1747, while in 1749 it was decreed that sodomy deserved a court martial and could be punished with death by hanging. Nevertheless one character in *Roderick Random* remarks that 'in our own country it gains ground apace, and in all probability will become in a short time a more fashionable vice than simple fornication'. It was also given a walk-on part in John Cleland's *Fanny Hill; or, Memoirs of a Woman of Pleasure* (1749), in which the heroine watches with mounting interest the antics of two young men. It has been suggested that Cleland himself was queer, transmogrifying adventures between men into ones between men and women. Ever the pornographer, he also includes the excitements between two women until the moment when Fanny eventually withdraws her hand 'wet and clammy'. From these books alone one might conclude that gay sex, for both males and females, was one of the readily available pleasures of the night.

But it was not necessarily free and easy. There were still many noblemen and gentlemen who fled to the Continent in order to avoid prosecution or obloquy; occasional panics over prosecution prompted many journeys over the sea, especially to Italy or to France. Edward Onslow went into exile at Clermont-Ferrand in 1781, for example, following an indiscretion at the Royal Academy with a London gentleman by the name of Phelim Macarty. The twin perils of disgrace and loneliness led many queers towards melancholy or despair. One such was Thomas Gray, the author of 'Elegy Written in a Country

Churchyard' (1750), whose naturally nervous disposition gave way to morbidity and anxious fear. He was well known for the flowers in his window boxes and the potpourri in his china vases, for the refinement of his dress and the delicacy of his manners, but nothing could ever be said about his secret. The sin, if such it was, lay deeply buried within him. It was for him a source of misery, as it must also have been for many of his contemporaries. Horace Walpole, one of Gray's dear friends, was also prey to fear and trembling. He wrote that 'I believe the state of my mind has contributed to a very weak and decaying body' and 'my present disorders'.

William Beckford was a dilettante and *littérateur* of a slightly later date whose romance *Vathek* (1782) had the added distinction of being composed in French. He began an affair with a sixteen-year-old, William Courtenay, and such was Beckford's distinction that it soon reached the public prints. The *Morning Herald* of 27 November 1784 commented that 'the rumour concerning a grammatical mistake of Mr B____ and the Hon. Mr C_____ in regard to the genders, we hope for the honour of nature originates in calumny!' The blanks in place of names of course fooled nobody in a city where everyone knew everyone else and where sexual preferences were endlessly discussed. Beckford left the country.

Another dilettante published a learned treatise on the subject of the erect penis. Richard Payne Knight's *Discourse on the Worship of Priapus and its Connection with the Mystic Theology of the Ancients* (1786) was in large part an enquiry into the fertility rites of pagans and Christians, together with diversions on such subjects as hermaphroditism and phallus worship. Christianity got the worst of it in arguments and learned footnotes. The book had been sponsored by the Society of Dilettanti but it was covertly a paean to same-sex activities.

Images of the phallus itself, as the holy grail of pagan ritual, were not to eighteenth-century taste. The book was attacked as 'containing all the ordure and filth, all the antique pictures and all the representations of generative organs in their most odious and degrading protrusion'. It was the kind of criticism, however, that might attract readers. Knight himself was banished from the clubs of London, and gained a perhaps unmerited reputation as a satyr in Georgian dress.

Another fashionable figure was the object of much vexed enquiry in the same period. The Chevalier d'Eon had lived as a male in France in his youth and early twenties but was then sent as a female spy to St Petersburg. On his return from Russia he began his military career as a captain of the dragoons before being sent to London in 1762 as Minister Plenipotentiary. He had professed himself mortified to be mistaken for a female, but then he confided to Beaumarchais that he was indeed a woman trapped in male clothes to serve the French state. He dressed as a female, and she dressed as a male. This was confusion incarnate. Within two months he appeared in the uniform of a captain of the French cavalry but at a later date emerged 'dressed in an elegant sack, her head-dress adorned with diamonds and bedecked with all the paraphernalia of her sex'. It was said that as a male he was petulant and somewhat irritable, but as a woman he was aggressive and boisterous. Casanova, the great connoisseur of sexuality, declared that 'I had not been a quarter of an hour in her company before I knew her for a woman'.

D'Eon travelled back to France in 1777 but then returned to London eight years later dressed as a woman, the role retained until his death in 1810. The atmosphere of London may have seemed to be more sympathetic. Bets about his sex, amounting to thousands of pounds, were taken in the London clubs and in the Stock Exchange. He was offered large sums to submit to physical examination, but he always refused. 'Man or woman?' d'Eon asked. 'I am none the better nor the worse.' It may be that d'Eon did not believe in two sexes at all, and that the concept of one sex was of more consequence. Is it possible that this figure comprised both sexes in some primordial mingling? Or did d'Eon live 230 years too soon for the transgender future?

Pressed for money, d'Eon eventually took up the role of female fencer, performing all over the country. The *Annual Register* remarked that 'it must be acknowledged that she is the most extraordinary person of the age', having been a spy, a diplomat, a soldier and an author of more than fifteen books. The French historian Jean de Lacretelle described d'Eon's life as one 'of much labour and suffering, mixed with very little repose'. D'Eon may have the last word, however. 'I have been the plaything of Nature . . . I have gone through all the strange vicissitudes of the human condition.'

When the body was laid out after death, it was discovered to be that of a man.

Of course d'Eon, Gray, Walpole and others were in a privileged position; they were not of the same rank as the subjects of scorn in *Satan's Harvest Home* (1749) which excoriated effeminate or effete young men for advancing the cause of sodomy. The anonymous author inveighs against 'vile catamites' who 'make their preposterous addresses, even in the very streets'. 'Instead of the pillory,' he writes (and one can only presume that it is a he), 'I would have the stake to be the punishment.'

But a spell in the pillory was often punishment enough. Women were generally part of the crowd that swore at and stoned the accused. Such women were given drink to refresh their strength, and were granted the best positions to take aim. A woman at one of these ritual stonings 'mounted the pillory, cut his breeches off, and flogged him until the blood came, and his head was broke in several places'. Two queer blackmailers, standing at Crutched Friars, 'were so severely treated by the mob, that it is thought they cannot recover'.

When in 1761 one man was placed in the pillory for attempting to have sex with a London apprentice, the mob grew so tumultuous that a child was killed in the crush. He had been surrounded by officers of the courts, but the crowd overpowered them before setting on the victim. In another incident of the same year, a victim was hauled 'round in the pillory so violently that, had not the board over his head been loose, his neck must have been broken. He fell down and lay for some time as dead; but they reared him up and set him on again where, covered with filth of all kinds, he remained some time, and then jumped down amongst the mob, who presently lifted him in again'.

The latter half of the eighteenth century was a harsh time. The *Public Advertiser* noted that 'a bugger aged sixty was put in the Cheapside pillory. The mob tore off his clothes, pelted him with filth, whipped him almost to death. He was naked and covered with dung. When the hour was up, he was carried almost unconscious back to Newgate.'

In the autumn of 1762 the master of a china shop, Mr Shann, asked to be transported for life rather than endure the punishment of the pillory. But his request was refused. When he was put on the wooden contraption at the upper end of Cheapside 'the populace then fell upon the wretch in the pillory, tore off his coat, waistcoat, shirt, hat, wig and breech, and then pelted and whipped him in a most severe manner'. A ballad was printed for the occasion, in which the women were portrayed as saying 'flog him!', 'here's a fair mark', 'cut it off'; one of them, hurling a piece of ripe fruit, called out 'take this buggume pear'. The victims sometimes died of their injuries before being taken down. Some were blinded. In the spring of 1780, after a particularly vicious episode, Edmund Burke rose in the House of Commons to lament this cruel punishment during which 'the poor wretch fell down dead on the stand of the instrument'. He had been too short to stand upright and therefore hung from the pillory by his neck. Burke added that the other man in the pillory 'was so maimed and hurt by what had been thrown at him, that he now lay without hope of recovery'. There were some attempts to bring the local officials to justice, but of course to no avail.

It was widely believed that the punishments fitted the crime. In William Blackstone's *Commentaries on the Laws of England* (1675–9) the jurist remarks that same-sex activity was 'of so dark a nature that the accusation if false deserves a punishment inferior only to the crime itself'; the crime was 'not fit to be named'. But it was named, not least in the courts. In a political journal, *Old England* (1750), it was stated that 'the Abomination is now notorious: our courts of justice have had it before them'. A great earthquake shook London in February 1750, and it was widely believed that it had been provoked by divine wrath against sodomitical sin.

It was considered to be contagious. When in 1760 a labourer attempted to assault a sixteen-year-old pupil of Dulwich College, the Crown counsel suggested that, had he been successful in committing 'this horrid and most detestable crime, he would have infected all the others'. It is not clear what the lawyer meant, other than to allude to the general anxiety that sodomy provoked. It was part of the urban darkness, as a witness testified in 1761. 'I am a butcher, my shop is in

Leadenhall market; as I come home from Leadenhall market, I come through the Cross-keys, there is a very dark passage. I have frequently run against men there, and I never could tell the reason for it.' He discovered the reason on the night of 28 July when 'I saw two bad men in a very indecent posture'. They were whispering. He entered his own house and beckoned to his servant. 'Do not go to bed, John. Follow me down. I believe there are a couple of very bad fellows in the alley.' The butcher and his servant 'laid hold' of the men until the watch was called. Another male couple were arrested for having sex in a coach along the Strand after dark; one of them, John Gill, was known locally as Miss Beasley. He had been dressed in a petticoat, satin shoes and silk stockings when he was taken. It cannot be known how many of these men were mistaken for women in the heat of the moment. 'Mollies' in this period also became known as 'madge mulls'.

Two eminent queers were given extraordinary publicity in 1772 in a number of London newspapers, from the *Daily Advertiser* to the *General Evening Post*. Thomas Jones, of the Royal Regiment or Artillery, was a figure in what was then known (albeit in a different sense) as 'the gay world'. He enjoyed appearing in masquerades. It can be inferred that masquerades were also occasions for the amorous male to seek out another of his kind. They were also the venue for male transvestites such as Princess Seraphina and Miss Beasley.

Francis Hay, thirteen years old, lived opposite 'Captain' Jones in St Martin's Court. Jones often noticed the boy, and gave him halfpence. One day in the summer of 1772 Jones came up to him and told him that he had a knee-buckle to be mended. He took the boy into his chambers where, as the boy testified, 'he pulled down my breeches and then his own . . . he set me in an elbow chair; he set me down and kissed me a little; then he made me lay down with my face on the chair, and so he came behind me; he put his cock into my bunghole'. The following day the boy reappeared and Jones 'made me rub his cock up and down till some white stuff came again'. Young Francis Hay was too ashamed to speak out, but was eventually convinced to do so. When he was asked why he had not protested sooner he replied that he thought his uncle would 'get business' out of it. The imperatives of trade were very strong in eighteenth-century London.

Jones was eventually sentenced to death, a verdict changed to transportation much to the disgust of the London crowd who were looking forward to a good hanging with all the trimmings. His case had become so well known that female prostitutes would call out 'Captain Jones! Captain Jones!', taunting any potential client who had scuttled off after rejecting their advances.

Another 'monster' or 'horrid wretch' or 'detestable and obnoxious beast', who shared the obloquy of 1772, was Samuel Drybutter. He was called in the press 'the celebrated toyman', by which was meant that he kept a stall selling watches and trinkets. But he was also believed to be the leader of the Macaroni Club. He was reported previously to have offered Jones a '*back* room' on the first floor with 'a convenient *back* door'. After the commutation of Jones's death sentence some of the public prints published an advertisement saying that 'Mr Dr-b-tt-r's club are desired to meet at the Gomorrhah, tomorrow evening, to consider of a proper address of thanks to the throne for the respite of brother Jones. The Macaroni, Dilettanti, and other Italian clubs will bring up the *rear* of the cavalcade, all dressed in *white linen breeches*.'

This juvenile humour spilled over in the street. It was now considered inadvisable to wear white trousers. Drybutter was now so well known that he was recognised, and became the object of public revenge. He had written that Jones should not have been condemned to death 'for his particular taste'. In one coffee house a customer poured chocolate over him, saying that this was 'his particular taste'; at another eating house he was basted with dripping, rolled in sawdust and covered in sauce. Eventually he moved to Paris to escape the mob.

'Suspicion gave birth to watchful observation,' the *Public Ledger* affirmed, 'and from a strict observation of Macaroni tribe . . . Take warning, therefore, ye smirking group of TIDDY DOLLS.' Macaronis were walking fashion plates who spoke and ate in an excessively fastidious manner; their hair was fashioned into beehives and pillars, which gave them a perpendicular Italian air. The *Oxford Magazine* of 1770 described the macaroni as 'neither male nor female, a thing of the neuter gender lately started up among us. It is called a macaroni. It talks without meaning, it smiles without pleasantry, it eats without appetite, it rides without exercise, it wenches without passion.' It was very queer indeed. The 'tiddy doll' was a junior version of the same tendency, perhaps derived from the phrase 'to tiddle' or to treat fondly. The supposed model was a gingerbread salesman who wore a gold suit, a laced hat with ostrich plume, a ruffled shirt and silk stockings. He also had a ready and caustic wit. Such overdressed eccentrics, bordering on queerness, were part of the panoply of London.

Other men were pursued by what might be known as vigilantes; the call went up in the streets of 'suck prick!' or 'cocksucker'. There are some cases of fellatio in the court records, but they are less frequent than references to sodomy or attempted sodomy. In *The Physiognomy of Mental Diseases* (1838), a pencil portrait of an alert if wary individual has a caption: 'Portrait of

J.T.D., aged forty . . . he was a day labourer, he had been insane for four years before his death, and was so much addicted to this unnatural vice that it was necessary to seclude him from other patients, who he continually annoyed; on one occasion the mouth of an idiot boy was the recipient: he died a few months ago of phthisis pulmonalis.'

It was a time, also, when disaffected servants might accuse their masters of attempted sexual abuse. Samuel Foote, a theatrical manager and comic performer, was in 1776 accused of assaulting his coachman, John Sangster, 'with an intent to commit buggery'. According to Sangster, Foote had recited all the benefits that his servant had received from him, including treatment for the measles, and added that 'the best recompense you can make is to let me have a fuck at you'. Fortunately for the accused, Sangster had muddled up his dates, and it was proved beyond doubt that Foote was not in town on the alleged occasion. Foote was acquitted but the strain of the trial may have been partly responsible for the stroke that killed him less than a year later. It should be mentioned that his noble and gentlemanly friends rallied around on the grounds that 'no man who kept male servants in his house would be safe from calumny'. How often, and how many, masters and servants were compromised is open to question.

It was still quite usual, however, for travellers to sleep with one another in the inns along the route of their journeys. One verse of the 1770s pointed the moral:

> Observe this rule – ne'er pull your breeches off,
> From health-restoring slumbers strive to keep,
> Or ten to one you are buggered in your sleep.

Richard Read was sharing a bed with Roger Sweetman in

the Crown of Lad Lane, when Sweetman tried to penetrate him. Read gave him 'two or three good pelts over the head' and said to 'take care for the future, never offer any such thing any more to any man, if you do you will get into a hobble'. 'Hobble' is no longer used, but its meaning is perfectly clear.

Better-natured encounters were recorded. William Procter, grocer, approached Thomas Readshaw, undertaker, with a question.

'What do you think of a good prick?'

'I don't do much in that way, but when I do, I have five guineas. But as I have taken a liking to you, I'll oblige you with two.'

They were caught *in flagrante*.

Of course rumour flourished at Whitehall and the court. Few politicians, especially those who remained unmarried, escaped without a verbal or pictorial whipping in the public prints. It was said of Pitt the Younger, for example, that he was 'stiff to everyone but a lady'. But the records suggest that the principal victims of the law were poor and unmarried. Sodomy was often associated with luxury and effeminacy but it could also be the companion of degradation and misery.

TRYING & PILLORING

of the

VERE STREET CLUB

Sold by J Brown No 1 Popes Head Court Quaker Street Spitalfields.

15

Rump riders

Public opinion in England seems to have turned against queers, male and female, by the 1790s. The German traveller Johann von Archenholz remarked that 'in no country are such infamous pleasures spoken of with greater detestation'. By the second decade of the nineteenth century, another traveller noted that 'the kiss of friendship between men is strictly avoided as inclining towards the sin regarded in England as more abominable than any other'.

This might perhaps have been the result of increasing numbers or increased visibility or, more likely, the consequence of that strict division between the sexes that became more and more prominent in the years leading to the Victorian ascendancy. Whatever the cause, male and female cross-dressing became much rarer by the late eighteenth century, as did the fashion for masquerade. Women should be women, and men should be men. It was possible to consider same-sex passion as a pathological condition pertaining to the individual. Where once it had been a question of acts that might or might not be prosecuted, now it was a question of persons with a distinct tendency to sin which might corrupt the neighbourhood.

Executions for sodomy reached a peak in the first decades of the nineteenth century, when over eighty men were hanged for the offence between 1806 and 1835. They were not all dispatched in London, since some of them were in the navy, but the city bore the brunt of prosecution and death. This was precisely the time when hanging for sodomy came to an end on the mainland of Europe and when in certain countries sexual relations between men were decriminalised. On the Continent no executions for the offence were carried out after 1791. In England they carried on with more vehemence. Its more ferocious penalties may in fact have been prompted by an effort to separate the country from Europe and, in particular, by moral panic at the prospect of a French invasion. The queers were the enemy within, upon whom public fears and anxieties could be directed. Homosexuality was a foreign vice. It was un-English. By 1810 many queers had been arrested, and the number was such that it led to openly expressed fears that the contagion was spreading out of control. The truth was that police surveillance had been increasing, leading in turn to more prosecutions, and to a clamour for further preventive measures. In 1810 the prisons were segregated between sodomites, apprentices and soldiers.

In 1808 Lord Liverpool, then the home secretary, ordered that the gates of Hyde Park and St James's Park be locked at night to 'prevent those scandalous practices in such a way that the public is kept ignorant of the disgrace of them'. This was a nineteenth-century variant of the medieval edict that sodomy was not to be named among Christians. The Vagrancy Act of 1824 had much the same purpose as the edict of Lord Liverpool. The police were allowed to arrest anyone 'wandering in the public streets or public highways, or in any place of public resort, and behaving in a riotous or indecent manner'. This could mean anything or nothing. It was a catch-all provision, very useful for those officers who suspected everything but could prove very little. The prosecutions for queer 'misdemeanours' now increased, and of course it was not unusual for the police to lure or entrap the unwary out of misplaced zeal or in the expectation of a bribe.

Patrick Colquhoun, stipendiary magistrate in Queen Square, had already taken preventive measures in 1806. He wrote to the magistrates urging them to keep special watch upon James Samuel Oliver Massey, or Miller, or Millwood, who 'had long been in the habit of seducing drum boys belonging to the King's Guards'. He was described as having 'something of the appearance of a decayed gentleman, wears a silver mounted eye glass suspended by a black ribbon round his neck . . . His greatest amusement is to attend military parades, where he never fails to use his glass in examining the appearance of the young men and drum boys.' The boys who succumbed to such advances were known as 'butterflies'. Some of these butterflies had eager admirers. William Beckford wrote to a friend in the autumn of 1807, 'if it is at all possible, go to see an angel called Saunders who is a tight-rope walker at the Circus Royal, and the certain captivator of every bugger's soul'.

Blackmailers flourished, and no doubt many queers were haunted by the prospect of the noose and the pillory. Some of the most exposed or most fearful fled from England.

Vere Street was located in Clare Market and the White Swan public house here, owned by James Cooke and others, had been secretly watched. When in the early summer of 1810 it was raided by officers of the court, twenty-three men were arrested – one was a butcher, one was a baker and another a lord. It was reported that the house had a room in which were several beds, a ladies' changing room, and a 'chapel' where marriages were celebrated. The officiating clergyman was one John Church, who was later accused of attempted sodomy, and in a further twist to an already extraordinary story it was reported that his friends had acted out the roles of attendant women and that at a supposed birth a pair of bellows had been used to expel a Cheshire cheese as the newborn. A century before, a wooden doll parodied the infant.

As soon as the cry went up that the men had been taken to Bow Street magistrates' court, a mob gathered outside the building and 'such was the fury of the crowd assembled', according to the *Morning Herald*, 'that it was with the utmost difficulty the prisoners could be saved from destruction'.

After they had been found guilty as charged, and before they were dispatched to prison, they were taken to the pillory guarded by one hundred mounted and one hundred unmounted policemen. 'Poor sods!' William Beckford, a keen observer of the proceedings, wrote. 'What a fine ordeal, what a procession, what a pilgrimage, what a song and dance, what a rosary!' A new pillory had been erected at Temple Bar, and the shops were closed for the occasion. 'Ammunition wagons' full of dead cats and turnip heads were driven by butchers' boys to the route.

By the time the men reached the Temple Bar, they had been punished enough. 'The first salute received by the offenders,' according to a contemporary report, 'was a volley of mud, and a serenade of hisses, hooting and execration, which compelled them to fall flat on their faces.' By the end of their journey, they resembled 'bears dipped in a stagnant pool . . . their faces were completely disfigured by blows and mud; and before they mounted, their whole persons appeared one heap of filth'. It was important to render them as pieces of excrement, in direct or indirect allusion to the physical conditions of their sexuality, so that they themselves became the crime. Two days previously a queer had been treated with equal brutality. A contemporary reported that 'the head of this wretch when he reached Newgate was compared to a *swallow's nest*'.

A pamphlet concerning the affair, *The Phoenix of Sodom, or, The Vere Street Coterie* (1813), emphasised the secrecy and ubiquity of the vice. 'How came a man of fortune and of fashion to such a house . . . even men in sacerdotal garb have descended

A sanitised depiction of a 'molly house' or male brothel. The interior would have been much less staged or staid, with foul smells, foul sights and the whole gamut of nineteenth-century sexuality. Male brothels were highly popular and even the children of the streets knew their locality.

The arrest of the Bishop of Clogher while engaged in dalliance with a soldier in the White Lion pub off the Haymarket. He fled to France but was known ever after as the 'arse-bishop'.

Charles Bannister dressed as Polly Peachum in John Gay's *The Beggar's Opera* (1781). 'Drag' parts are as old as the theatre itself, and have always been a favourite of gay audiences.

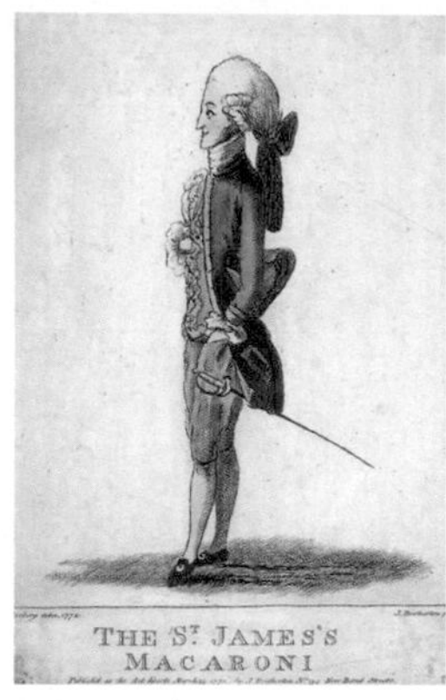

A St James's macaroni, one who dressed in a flamboyant and effeminate manner to emphasise his distinction from the rough male world.

The Chevalier d'Eon was a mystery wrapped in an enigma, sometimes appearing as a man and sometimes as a woman. He dressed as a young woman to act as a French spy at the Russian court but then on his return to France served as the commander of a company of dragoons. Bets were taken on the nature of his sex and money was inevitably lost when, on his death, he was discovered to be a male.

Two Victorian queers, Ernest Boulton and Frederick Park, were arrested outside the Strand Theatre in 1870. They were popularly known as Stella and Fanny and dressed in fashionable female attire in order to attract male attention in various places of gay resort.

Oscar Wilde, once the triumph of London society, became its pariah. His liking for lower-class boys, despite the fact that his predilections were widely shared, proved to be his undoing.

Tite Street, the home of Oscar Wilde and his wife Constance, which after his conviction was stripped of its books and furniture.

E. M. Forster did not care to assert his homosexuality in public, even though he practised it in private, but he left his own testament to gay love in a novel, *Maurice*, which was not published until after his death.

Radclyffe Hall wrote about gay women in *The Well of Loneliness* (1928), a novel which provoked immense public disapproval. The chief magistrate, at a subsequent trial, denounced it as an 'obscene libel' but it was not clear where the libel lay. The novel itself is now regarded as one of the pioneering texts of lesbian literature.

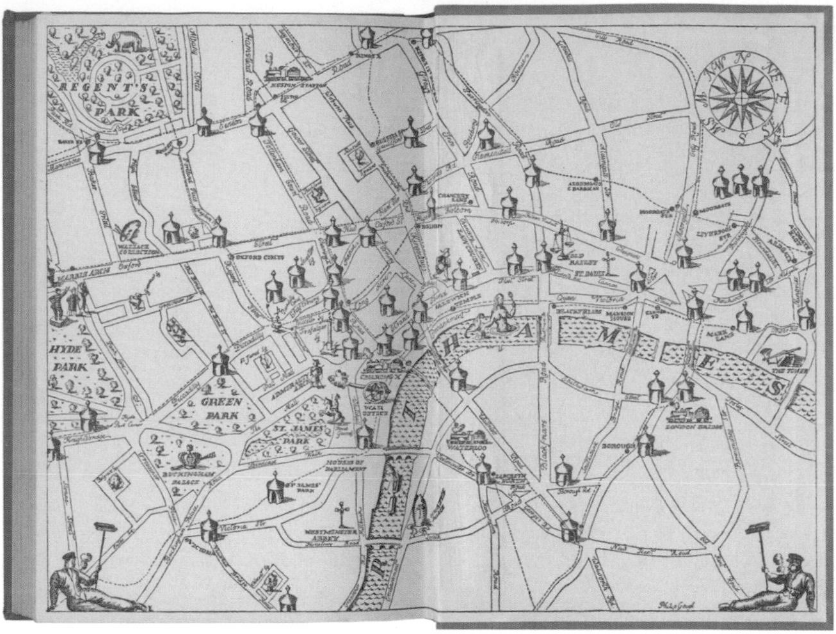

A map of the locality of London's lavatories for Paul Pry's *For Your Convenience: A Learned Dialogue Instructive to all Londoners and London Visitors, Overheard at the Theleme Club and Taken Down Verbatim* (1937). It proved to be a Baedeker for gays, foreign and domestic, as they confronted alluring choices.

A shadowy Piccadilly in 1955, well known as the home of furtive sexual pleasures for unaccompanied men. It was a Mecca for London gays in the twentieth century and beyond.

Sir John Wolfenden was the principal author of the report, published in 1957, which recommended the decriminalisation of homosexuality. It was one of the beacons for the wave of toleration in the sixties.

Quentin Crisp turned homosexuality into an art by playing himself on stage and television. He was the first modern queer who took great pride in his status.

The dramatist Joe Orton was the epitome of what came to be known as 'rough trade'. He was an habitué of public lavatories and liked working-class encounters which he recorded in his enthralling diaries.

The actor Sir John Gielgud was one of the victims of police oppression when, in 1953, he was arrested for 'cruising' in a public lavatory. He was fined but, on returning to the stage a few days later, he was given a standing ovation.

The Biograph, or 'Bio-Grope', a cinema of first resort for London gays who now had the pleasure of soliciting in comfort. The film did not matter.

An OutRage! protest. The movement was established in 1990 to affirm the right of queer people to their 'sexual freedom, choice and self-determination'.

The interior of Gateways, the most illustrious and popular of all clubs for gay women. Its famous 'green door' did not close until 1985.

A protest against the Blasphemy Laws in 1977 under which the publisher of *Gay News* was given a suspended sentence for printing a gay poem about Jesus.

Protesters ride past Trafalgar Square on a pink tank at Pride in 1995.

A couple celebrates at a Pride march in 2007.

The Soho nightclub Madame JoJo's was shut down after a violent altercation in 2014.

The Campaign for Equal Marriage is dedicated to treating same-sex marriages as valid and equal under the law.

A Soho vigil held in the aftermath of the attack on the queer night-club Pulse in Orlando, Florida in 2016.

from the pulpit to the gully-hole of breathing infamy in Vere Street.' The 'gully-hole' is a reference to other holes. This mudbath of horrors was further polluted by the mingling of the classes. 'Men of rank, and of respectable situations in life, might be seen wallowing in or on the beds with wretches of the lowest description.' One of these was a chimney sweep and another a 'nightman', who swept the shit from the streets, 'an employment not ill appropriate to the delicate passions of which constitute his amusement'. One respectable gentleman of the City 'stayed several days and nights together; during which time he generally amused himself with eight, ten and sometimes a dozen different boys and men . . . It is said that this animal is now in a mad-house.' The author of the diatribe, Robert Holloway, mentioned one 'sink' in Blackman Street off Borough High Street, another by the Obelisk in St George's Fields and a third in Bishopsgate Street.

William Beckford christened the area around Seven Dials, in the poorest part of London, the 'Holy Land' in obvious reference to the waifs and strays who could be purchased there; it does not throw a favourable light upon his character as an exploiter of the poor. He made a similar remark upon Hounslow Heath, an area where he might pick up 'roughs'; he had declared that he had 'such favourite ideas about the site of Hounslow that I couldn't ask for any other Paradise'. Religiosity and sexuality seem to have been strangely confused.

There was another consequence of the Vere Street affair. Two of those taken up at the Swan were a drummer boy and an ensign; they were separately arraigned and convicted towards the end of the year and were both sentenced to be hanged outside the debtors' door of Newgate prison. It was reported that several prominent individuals were among the crowd watching the spectacle and one of these interested observers, according to *The Times*, was the Duke of Cumberland, whose valet had been murdered eight months before in what detectives call suspicious circumstances; the unlicensed press suggested that the killing had been used to cover up the duke's unnatural liaison with another servant. It was reported that 'the ghost of White, the drummer boy, lately executed for sodomy, pays his nocturnal visits to old Moggy, the rump-rider, Park Street'. The reference is to a queer haunt known as Moggy Stewart's.

The Duke of Cumberland later became King of Hanover, where he presided over a gay court. Other queers were not so fortunate. Lord Courtenay, who was supposed to have been involved with William Beckford, was strongly advised to depart for France. He had said that none of his fellow peers would convict him because they were 'like himself'. But he was quickly disabused. No lord would willingly step forward in his defence. He stayed in Paris for the rest of his life.

In 13 January 1811, a university friend of Byron, Charles Skinner Matthews, wrote to the poet that 'the grand feature, I take it, in the last year of our history, is the enormous increase of paederestia . . . At no place or time I suppose, since the creation of the world, has sodomy been so rife . . . every news[paper] that one casts one's eyes upon, presents one with some instance.' Byron was at the time in Malta, and Matthews adds that 'what you get for five pounds we must risk our necks for'.

Byron, who had more to fear than most, told his half-sister, Augusta, that 'even to have such a thing said is utter destruction and ruin to a man, and from which he can never recover'. He himself recollected that 'I was abused in the public prints, made the common talk of private companies, hissed as I went to the House of Lords, insulted in the streets, afraid to go to the theatre . . .' In the autumn of 1816 one sodomite, standing on the scaffold and facing the rope, told his confessor that he wished to make a full confession with names and dates. The worthy Anglican divine, Father Cotton, replied smoothly, 'My dear Sir, better not, better not.' Beckford, hearing of this, called the clergyman, 'stupid, hypocritical, bloodthirsty vermin!' It was clear that the condemned man was about to name those in high places.

In the same year General Sir Eyre Coote was found guilty of paying the boys of Christ's Hospital to beat him, and for him to beat them in turn while they were 'stretched upon a long low table for the purpose'. He sometimes used an instrument and sometimes his bare hand. His military colleagues testified that his behaviour 'proceeded from insanity alone'. But that did not save him from dishonour; he was removed from the Army List and stripped of the Order of the Bath. The boys themselves were not necessarily innocents in danger. Public schools were generally believed to 'wallow in filth' and the first words that William Makepeace Thackeray heard when entering his dormitory at the age of eleven was 'Come and frig me'.

One significant figure in the period protested against the general barbarity and hypocrisy of the sodomy laws. Jeremy Bentham's doctrine of utilitarianism, stripped of its subtleties, asks: what is this action good for? Does it increase the sum of human happiness? He applied these questions to the sodomy laws of England in the full and certain belief that he would be attacked and slandered. 'Miscreant!' he imagined his opponents screaming, 'you are one of them then!' In 1774 he had written some notes on reform of the law, citing precedents from the Enlightenment and classical antiquity. By 1818 he had composed a 500-page treatise in which he urged that the morally slandered men and women of England should be left alone. The 'bonds of attachment' in male love are good and useful in their own right. What is bad, useless and reprehensible is the amount of cruelty, violence and mischief perpetrated against same-sex lovers. He described one hanging judge; 'delight and exultation glistened in his countenance, his looks called for applause and congratulations at the hands of the surrounding audience'. It is a vision worthy of Fuseli.

Bentham argued with his own abrasive good sense. 'It seems rather too much to subscribe to men's being hanged to save the indecency of enquiring whether they deserve it . . . do not exhaust your invention to belabour it with hard names but point out and ascertain with calmness and perspicuity the specie and proportion of misery it occasions.' He stated, perhaps for the first time, that sodomy 'is a crime, if a crime it is to be called, that produces no misery in society'. He added that 'bad taste is a very bad reason for a man's being thrust into perdition with the vilest, and that to thirst after a man's blood who is innocent, if innocence consists in the doing of no harm to anyone, is a much worse taste'.

To utter such sentiments in public would be to throw into jeopardy all his moral, social and philosophical work. If he touched the subject he would do so, as he said, 'with a halter about his neck'. His work was never published in his lifetime.

It is extremely unlikely, however, that if it had been published it would have made the slightest difference to the rigour of the law. The appetite for sensation and the desire for punishment were so strong that no force on earth could have withstood them.

In 1822 the Bishop of Clogher entertained and excited public discourse. On the evening of Friday 19 July a young soldier in the Foot Guards, John Moverley, entered the White

Lion Tavern in Charles Street off the Haymarket before taking a pint of porter into the back parlour. He was joined a few minutes later by the Bishop of Clogher, dressed in his clerical garb. The good bishop had a history. He was a prominent member of the Society for the Suppression of Vice.

The presence of the bishop and the soldier aroused the suspicions of the landlord and his son. They crept around the back and, through a window, saw the two men engaged in some kind of sexual activity. It is not clear from the record who was buggering whom. The landlord called together his customers and they all burst into the parlour where cleric and soldier had their breeches around their ankles. The watch was called.

On their journey to the watch-house the two men were manhandled by the mob who jeered at them and tore their clothes. It was not often the crowd had a bishop in its clutches. It seems that he was still wearing gentlemanly clerical garb because he had come directly from the House of Lords.

The following morning, at the Marlborough Street police station, both men refused to reveal their identities. But the bishop managed to scribble a note to a dependant. 'John – come to me directly, don't say who I am, but I am undone.' The relevant sureties were given for the bishop and, since he had been given professional advice while in custody, he was granted bail of one thousand pounds without revealing his name. The soldier was somehow spirited away the next day so that he might avoid interrogation. Yet no secret lasts in London. Soon it became common knowledge that the Lord Bishop of Clogher was a bugger. It also became clear that he had been allowed to escape the law by means of a sizeable bail, emphasising the fact that even in the case of sodomy two laws were practised – one for the rich and the other for the poor. A squib was circulated.

> The Devil to prove the Church was a farce
> Went out to fish for a Bugger.
> He bated his hook with a Frenchman's arse
> And pulled up the bishop of Clogher.

Clogher became known as the 'Arse-Bishop'. He fled to Paris, but ended his life as an anonymous butler in Edinburgh. The private secretary to Robert Peel, then the home secretary, took a more sober view of the fiasco. 'No event in the last century,' he wrote, 'is more to be lamented both on private and public grounds – it will sap the very foundation of society . . .'

It was possibly as a result of the Clogher scandal that the foreign secretary, Lord Castlereagh, committed suicide by cutting his throat. It was widely believed and reported that the severe anxiety and overwork, which were then the inevitable lot of the ministers of the Crown, had turned his wits, causing what at a later date would be called a 'nervous breakdown'. He had indeed broken down, but perhaps not for the reasons provided.

It seems that he was tormented by the belief that he was being, or was about to be, blackmailed for homosexuality. He was under the delusion (if it was indeed a delusion) that he had been seen entering a male brothel. He was marked out. He would never be clean again; he would never be safe again. He is reported to have confessed his sexual indiscretions to his physician, to his wife, and to a society hostess, Harriet Arbuthnot. In his mania he told the king that he was being accused of Clogher's crime, and George IV became concerned for the minister's sanity. Some peculiarities emerged. Castlereagh insisted that he was being blackmailed but resisted any advice to inform the police; he wanted to spare his wife the indignity, although eventually he committed the greater shame of self-murder. It remains an open question, not helped by the fact that his corpse was jeered when it was laid in Westminster Abbey. It is likely that Castlereagh wished to avoid an explosive political scandal at the cost of his own life.

It was well known that any case of sodomy involving those of a higher social class attracted large crowds to the court-rooms. Many in the dock tried hard to conceal their rank by dressing as footmen, servants or labourers, and used every legal means to avoid revealing their true identity. As one solicitor put it, 'you have a name given, and there is not a particle of evidence that this is not the real name of the prisoner. In the absence of evidence to the contrary, you are bound to suppose that the prisoner has given his real name.' The more wealthy suspects might also bribe the penny-a-line court reporters to conceal their names.

Soldiers were not only in demand from bishops. Guardsmen were known to congregate at the White Lion Tavern. Soldiers released from duty on Horse Guards Parade were accustomed to meeting at the Rose and Crown in St Martin's Lane, as well as the Bull and the Barley Mow in the Strand. The evenings in the Barley Mow were known as 'free and easies', where soldiers and clients danced cheek to cheek. The soldiers from Knightsbridge Barracks also frequented the local pubs for passing trade, while another barracks provided the attraction for a trysting place in Orange Street just behind the newly built National Gallery.

A correspondent of Havelock Ellis amplified the reports by noting that 'choirboys reinforce the ranks to a considerable extent, and private soldiers to a large extent. Some of the barracks (notably Knightsbridge) are great centres. On summer evenings Hyde Park and the neighbourhood of Albert Gate is full of guardsmen and others plying a lively trade, and with little disguise, in uniform or out . . . It is worth noting that there is a perfect understanding in this matter between soldiers and the police, who may always be relied upon by the former for assistance and advice.' It is not clear what assistance or advice was required.

The small alleys between Orange Street and Trafalgar Square became notorious to the extent that one man in the vicinity was deemed to have been 'roaming about for some unexplained motive' suggesting that 'his conduct is in that respect suspicious'. Some areas became so popular in the early years of the nineteenth century that placards were pasted on the walls. 'Beware of Sods!' If a customer wished to avoid the inconvenience of casual encounters, a famous brothel of underage boys could be found in Spitalfields during the early 1830s. Boys were also placed for auction under the railway viaduct in White Street; the curls beside their ears were known as 'Newgate knockers'.

The largest incidence of crime relating to sexual matters, in the early nineteenth century, was concerned with extortion and blackmail. In an age of suspicion it was the most profitable. A Threatening Letters Act was passed in 1825 but there was never an end to accusers.

One of the most curious cases involved picture-shop windows. John Muirhead, a queer who was nevertheless a member of the Society for the Suppression of Vice, struck up a conversation with a young man outside a shop that displayed sporting prints and other memorabilia; one remark led to another, and it so happened that Muirhead always carried in his pocket prints of a licentious nature which were the early-nineteenth-century equivalent of dirty photographs. He also took out two 'skins', or condoms, and asked the young man if he could fill them. At a later date he took three boys to the second floor of an oyster shop where he took advantage of their inflamed passions by showing them 'prints of the most indecent and shocking nature' before having his way with them. On one of his forays a print-shop owner in Holywell Street dangled a print of the Bishop of Clogher through the window in front of him, in order to scare him away, but the gesture had no effect. Muirhead was eventually arrested and sentenced to fifteen months' imprisonment.

He could not have chosen more satisfactory premises for his dirty prints. Holywell Street, off the Strand, was well known for its indecent and pornographic works, many of which concerned gay sex. There were supposed to be fifty-seven pornography shops in as many yards, perhaps an exaggeration, and the *Daily Telegraph* condemned the sight of young people of both sexes 'furtively peering in at these sin-crammed shop windows'.

Other, better connected, men were allowed to evade the consequences of the law. William Bankes, the Member of Parliament for Dorset, was in 1833 found 'standing behind the screen of a place for making water against Westminster Abbey walls, in company with a soldier named Flower, and of having been surprised with his breeches and braces unbuttoned at ten at night, his companion's dress being in similar disorder'. After a parade of eminent witnesses testified on his behalf the MP was found to be not guilty. The foreman of the jury stated that Bankes left the court without a stain – to which an observer added 'on his shirt'. The fate of Flower is unknown. But eight years later Bankes was arrested in a similar situation, with a guardsman in Green Park; he left the country.

*

John Sparshott, aged nineteen, was strung up in August 1835 and, according to one newspaper account, the old custom of passing the hands of the dead man over the necks of two or three women was still in use 'as a supposed cure for glandular enlargements'. Three months later John Smith and John Pratt were suspended outside Newgate prison for the same offence. They had the distinction, if such it was, of being the last men sentenced to death for buggery in England. They were poor men, both of them married, who had been found in a derelict boarding house on the south bank of the Thames. The magistrate, Henry Wedgwood, stated that 'the detection of these degraded creatures was owing entirely to their poverty; they were unable to pay for privacy, and the room was so poor that what was going on inside was easily visible from without'. It was a miserable location, and a miserable end, with all the sorrow of London somewhere within it. Queer men under sentence of death were in every sense pariahs; when Captain Nichols was hanged in 1833 no member of his family approached him or appealed for a lighter sentence. He went to his death unmourned. The death penalty for buggery was abolished in 1861, when the punishment was replaced by that of penal servitude for life. Sexual assaults of other kinds warranted a sentence of three months to two years.

In 1829 a carpenter, James Allen, was killed in an industrial accident. He had earned his living in the trade for twenty-one years, and seemed to be happily married. At the coroner's inquest, however, it was discovered to general surprise that Allen was in fact female.

Four years later the body of Lavinia or Eliza Edwards, then unwanted and unclaimed, was taken up from the streets and dispatched to Guy's Hospital for dissection. It was there discovered to be that of a young male and, according to the subsequent report, 'the state of the rectum left no doubt of the abominable practices to which this individual had been addicted'. Eliza had been a performer in female roles who had toured the country, and was known by erstwhile friends as a 'very lady-like woman'. After her theatrical career had come to an end, she had taken to the streets. The delicate situation of posing as a member of the other sex was well understood in this period, as a verse from 'The Rummy Cove's Delight' of 1833 illustrates.

Ye wives when you marry of course you expect
That your husband with something in front will be decked;
And should he be gifted with what's rather small,
It's better than if he had nothing at all.
But the story I tell you is true, on my life,
It's found out a woman has married a wife
Who was strong, who was hearty, was stout and was tall
But to please her poor spouse she had – Nothing at all.

The Sinks of London, published two years later, tried variations on the same theme. It purports to be a journalist's account of a cheap lodging house in Seven Dials which, of the poor addresses in London, was close to being the poorest and the most abandoned. This was the neighbourhood where many people lost hope. One 'creature' lodging there was between four and five feet in height with one leg longer than the other. He wore a 'flash' coat and a female shawl, and so his appearance was perplexing. He looked like 'a masculine woman and sounded like a man'; he 'swaggered around the room, his hat half pulled over his brows, and slouched a little on one side; assuming that scowling look of a bully, and at times the flashy air of a gallant'. Her sex, however, was well known to her neighbours.

Another queer fellow appeared before the magistrates of Hatton Garden. The magistrate, Mr Bennett, asked for the name.

PRISONER (speaking in a rough manner): It is Mary Chapman.
MR BENNETT: I never saw a figure more like a man, and the voice is manly.
WITNESS: I have known her at least ten years and she always appears in a dress similar to the one she now wears, namely, a hat, smock-frock, trousers or knee breeches . . .
MR BENNETT: She may be a disorderly and disreputable character, which, in fact, her dressing as a man clearly shows, but I know of no law to punish her for wearing male attire . . . I advise you to be careful. If I could punish you, I would.

The tradition of the Jacobean 'roaring girl' was in fact very much alive. Mary Newall, known as 'The Artful Girl of Pimlico', was in 'the habit of stealing out to low theatres alone, hiring cabs to go in, and smoking cigars with the cabmen'.

THE SINS
OF THE
CITIES OF THE PLAIN
OR THE
RECOLLECTIONS OF A MARY-ANN

WITH SHORT ESSAYS ON

SODOMY AND TRIBADISM

IN TWO VOLUMES

VOLUME I.

LONDON
PRIVATELY PRINTED
1881

16

Omi-palone

In 1855 a thoroughly modern guidebook was published for the demi-monde of England with particular reference to the lower depths of what was called 'little Lunnon'; *The Yokel's Preceptor: or, More Sprees in London!* was 'every swankey's book' and 'the greenhorn's guide' of 'flymy kens and flash cribs', the terminology of which was to be deciphered in 'a Joskin's vocabulary' 'of the various slang words now in constant use'. Among them were of course 'margery', 'poof', 'backgammon' and other words of queer derivation. It was important for the yokels to find a 'way to know the beasts'. It might even be described as a guide to queer London without drawing undue attention to the fact.

The 'beasts' could be seen at the southern and eastern ends of Regent Street, in Fleet Street, the Strand and among the purlieus of Charing Cross. Nowhere was safe. The Burlington Arcade had become a nest of male whores, where you could find 'a bit of brown' or some 'back-door work'. The Alhambra Theatre was similarly to be avoided. The London Pavilion and the bar of the St James's Hotel were 'so', in the word of the time, as was a skating rink in Knightsbridge. Two public houses, the Crown on Charing Cross Road and the Windsor Castle on the Strand, were eminent. It is perhaps significant that the queer quarters of London had finally reached the West End, leaving most of the City behind, emphasising that sexual culture followed or accompanied consumer culture. That was where the money, and the customers, and the bright lights, were all to be found. The old signs, however, still seemed to be in use. 'When they see what they imagine to be a chance, they place their fingers in a peculiar manner underneath the tails of their coats, and wag them about – the method of giving the office.'

This may have something to do with the contemporary rise of the great metropolis of which queers were an integral part. The pertinent characteristics of a large city such as London – the railway termini (even the trains themselves), the public baths, the arcades, the parks, the museums and art galleries, the gymnasia, the restaurants, the new theatres, the public lavatories and above all the restless streets – formed the perfect environment for same-sex pursuits.

In 1854 a transvestite ball at the Druids' Hall in Turnagain Lane was raided. One of its participants, a man of sixty, was arrested; he was 'dressed in the pastoral garb of a shepherdess of the golden age'. 'Drag' entered the vocabulary in the 1860s, and has never left it since. When George Paddon was arrested on the Hackney Road in the summer of 1863, the constable testified that his abnormally large crinoline was the only clue. Paddon was also wearing a silk dress with an 'over dress' as well as a lady's French coat trimmed with black lace. But the policeman stated that 'he should never have taken her for a man but for the crinoline', a response that elicited from the members of the court 'uncontrollable laughter'.

In April 1864 one prurient diarist, Arthur Munby, came upon an advertisement for a ball at a pleasure garden in Camberwell. The tickets were selling at a shilling each, a relatively expensive sum, and Munby set out to investigate the clientele. He realised that 'not a few of the youths were elaborately disguised as women of various kinds; some so well that only their voices showed they were not girls – and pretty girls. This is a new thing to me, and is simply disgusting.'

If many Londoners were unaware of male cross-dressing except as an act in the penny gaffs or pantomimes, the unexpected appearance of two young men in the dock at Bow Street magistrates' court came as a revelation. One wore a cherry-pink evening dress trimmed with lace, while the other was dressed in dark green satin with a shawl of the same material. Ernest Boulton and Frederick Park, otherwise known as Stella and Fanny, were accused of 'conspiring and inciting persons to commit an unnatural offence'. They had been arrested, while wearing the same female clothes, at the Strand Theatre in the spring of 1870. In a contemporary pamphlet to celebrate the occasion of the trial it was revealed that at the theatre 'the ladies leaned over their box, twirled their handkerchiefs, and lasciviously ogled the male occupants of the stalls'.

It soon transpired at the Bow Street hearings that the two young men were well known for their transvestite escapades in the West End. They had been thrown out of the Alhambra Theatre in Leicester Square for exhibitionism and making 'chirruping' sounds to attract male attention. The manager testified that 'they were looking in front of the box, handing cigarettes backwards and forwards to each other, and lighting them by gaslight'. They were frequent visitors to the Burlington Arcade, where the beadle knew them well; he was addressed by them as 'you sweet little dear'. They had been seen, *en travesti*, at the Casino in Holborn, at fancy-dress balls at Haxell's Hotel and the Royal Exeter Hotel, and, curiously enough, at the Oxford and Cambridge Boat Race. It seemed that any crowd of males would draw them out. They made a habit of parading down Regent Street, the Quadrant and the Haymarket. They had been seen to wink and pout at gentlemen while Stella used to turn her head 'in a sly manner'. They were, in truth, importuning, like any other prostitute, male or female.

On the day of their arrest they had been followed by police agents in their pursuit of what was called 'frippery and frivolity'. They had travelled by cab to Oxford Street, for example, where they purchased gloves and then to Portland Place in order to buy jewellery. The law finally pounced at the Strand Theatre.

The police called in a surgeon to examine the two defendants, but it subsequently appeared that the doctor had been overenthusiastic in his work by initiating a rectal examination which was later denounced as a 'revolting procedure'. The attorney general commented at the trial that 'fortunately there is very little learning . . . upon this subject in this country'. The police and doctors, in other words, did not know what they were doing.

In defence of Fanny and Stella their barrister claimed that they were simply theatrical, albeit to an extraordinary degree, and that they considered their activities to be a bit of a 'lark'. They had even appeared, as actresses, in minor theatres and village halls where they had been applauded to the echo. Boulton's mother testified that her son 'had dressed up as a girl from the age of six. As a child his favourite role was that of parlour maid, in which he deceived his own relations.' It was all very English.

They were not considered to be sodomites or blackmailers, although in truth they may indeed have dabbled in those activities. No one was harmed, and in fact very few people were offended. The London public took their side; they were applauded whenever they left the magistrates' court and their testimony was greeted with gales of laughter. Despite the strictures of the moralists, it was all just good fun. From the evidence of the press reports, the London crowd was quite accustomed to 'drag' on the streets of the city. The city was known in that sense to be free and easy.

The magistrates' hearings were followed by a trial at Westminster Hall in the spring of the following year but much of the material about cross-dressing and prostitution was omitted. The earlier reports about large gatherings of queer men at gay parties were also omitted. It seemed that too much had already been said, and none of the legal teams wished to leave the impression that London was a queer Eldorado.

The confused evidence of the police and others, as well as the botched surgical examination, led to the prosecution being dropped. The jury found the two men not guilty of conspiring to commit a felony, whereupon Stella fainted. He had by now grown a moustache. Clean-shaven men were in this period an object of constant suspicion.

Some relatively sensational letters had been read out in court. Stella had written to an erstwhile admirer that 'I am consoling myself in your absence by getting screwed'. Fanny had complained of the weather that 'it has turned so showery that I can't get out without a dread of my back hair coming out of curl'. He had also alluded to 'my campish undertakings'. 'Camp' was so new a word that one newspaper interpreted it as 'craw-fish'. Another phrase worth remarking on, 'we shall come in drag', marks the first time that the word 'drag' was heard in a court of law. Another letter from a witness included the phrase that 'I care for nothing but trade'. But the meaning here of 'trade' was too much for a court of law.

This was one province of the queer world from which emerged the queer slang known as 'polari', a strange amalgam of Romany, Yiddish, lingua franca, cockney rhyming slang, back slang and vagrants' canting terms that were as ancient as vagrants themselves. A 'huge cartzo' was a large penis, 'lallies' were legs and a 'bona ecaf' was a nice face. 'Omi' was a man and 'omi-palone' an effeminate man; 'martinis' were hands and 'aunt nells' were ears. 'Dona' or 'palone' was a woman; and at a later date 'sharpy palone' was a policewoman. It all became, in the language of polari, very 'camp'. In the twentieth century polari was a familiar and frequently used 'other' language as a secret code to disguise the often sexual meanings of various words; thus it was employed in theatres, pantomimes and the merchant navy. It afforded a sense of community and belonging among those who spoke it, and sealed them off from the various impositions of the common language. 'Naff' was one of the words that crossed the divide, but 'national handbag', the dole, did not. It was, in a sense, the language of the suppressed. But by the beginning of the twenty-first century it was rarely employed.

It is a short step from the dance floor or the shopping arcade to the workhouse or the dosshouse. Some queer men actively sought out those of a lower class. It afforded them more satisfaction. It was not necessarily a question of power, although that might play a part. The man or boy could turn out to be a brutal blackmailer, in front of whom the most experienced queer might quail. It was essentially a question of money. In a culture dominated more and more by commodities, the body was one of the most delectable.

John Addington Symonds, a poet and critic of the latter half of the nineteenth century, was inclined to metropolitan wanderings. On one of his journeys through the city he glimpsed a graffito that seemed to him to be 'so thoroughly the voice of vice and passion in the proletariat that it pierced the very marrow of my soul'. The graffito in question was, in his words, 'of phallic meeting, glued together gushing'. The legend beneath it was 'prick to prick, so sweet'.

This crudely drawn scene overwhelmed Symonds, eliciting a furious hunger for sensation of a similar kind. He had once before rejected the advances of a soldier with a mixture of fascination and revelation. Now he picked up a guardsman and took him to a brothel. For him it was wonderful to touch, and even to converse with, a member of the lower class. No doubt for the soldier it was simply business as usual.

Guardsmen appear in many reminiscences of the period, where they are treated as synonymous with male prostitutes. They could be found everywhere in London at a price ranging from four shillings to a sovereign. One middle-aged guardsman admitted that he and his colleagues used to 'break in' the raw recruits, but he added that most young men did not need any preparatory training. Elder brothers or older friends had done their duty in advance. He added that 'although of course we all do it for money, we do it because we really like it, and if gentlemen gave us no money, we should do it all the same'. Those in the upper ranks were not immune from suspicion. It was widely reported that Field Marshal Kitchener and Major General Sir Hector Macdonald were 'so'.

The murder of a homosexual artist, Archibald Wakley, dominated the sensational press in the spring of 1906. The young painter was in the habit of inviting soldiers to his studio, where they might of course pose as models, but his artistic career came to an end when his body was found fatally slashed and his skull cracked open. Certain details were left unrecorded in the press, including the fact that marks on his thighs had been made by the spurs worn by the Royal Horse Guards. He might have been ridden to death.

There was a large market for those who were attracted to the poor. The connection between homelessness and same-sex activity was customarily made in the latter half of the nineteenth century; George Orwell would testify at a later date that the tramp had the reputation for being queer. This might in part be explained by the association with vagrancy and the Vagrancy Act, but there is evidence that the solitary wandering life of the tramp encouraged homosocial longings. If homelessness and homosexuality were intimately linked, it was part of an urban history in which tramps openly favoured boys as sexual companions. Another type of family might thus be established. The vagrant havens known collectively as Rowton House, in Whitechapel, King's Cross, Newington Butts and elsewhere, were also well known for illicit activities. In a world of loneliness and comfortless privation the need for human warmth and human sympathy were every bit as important as food and drink. The 'refuges' where the homeless were taken in for the night were reported to be havens for queer sex, and some well-to-do gentlemen disguised themselves as vagrants in order to gain entry.

John Addington Symonds professed more delicate motives. 'I have never been able to understand,' he wrote, 'why people belonging to different strata of society – if they love each other – could not enter into comradeship.' Comrade was the just word. It implied masculine fraternity which could also provide the proper motive for an enlarged philanthropic activity.

Three articles in the *Pall Mall Gazette* of January1866, were entitled 'A Night in the Workhouse' and were set in the casual ward of Lambeth Workhouse. The journalist, Frederick Greenwood, professed himself to have experienced 'the fate of Sodom'. Here were mingled on single bunk beds 'great bulking ruffians', homeless juveniles and 'dirty scoundrels' engaged in any and every form of sexual intercourse; Greenwood lay and listened in the dark to 'infamous' noises. He described the place as a male brothel designed for the 'hideous' pleasures of the poor and the destitute, but added as a grace note the presence of a handsome youth whose cropped hair 'looked soft and silky; he had large blue eyes set wide apart, and a mouth that would have been faultless but for its great width'. The boy picked his way lightly among the beds asking 'Who'll give me part of his doss . . . who'll let me turn in with him?' Greenwood feared 'how it would be'. This was the fate of London's victims. The articles caused much outrage and consternation among those who did not know that the lower depths of the city could be quite so dark. Two weeks later reporters from the *Daily News* visited the same workhouse and discovered 'youths lay in the arms of men, men were enfolded in each others' embraces . . . the air was laden with a pestilential stench'.

Other public refuges concealed shadowy practices. Dr Barnardo, who entitled one of his reports on poor children *Rescue the Perishing*, was accused of 'stripping children of their proper clothing, cutting their clothes, and dressing them in rags, for the purpose of getting up fictitious and deceptive photographs'. This brand of poverty porn was manufactured deliberately on the understanding that underdressed or half-naked children might evoke an erotic as well as a charitable response.

The general fears and suspicions about London, by those inclined to fear and suspicion, were amply confirmed by the publication in 1881 of *The Sins of the Cities of the Plain*. It was about one city, of course, and this city was by no means situated on level ground. It was subtitled 'The Recollections of a Mary-Ann, with Short Essays on Sodomy and Tribadism', the 'Mary-Ann' or queer in question being a young prostitute by the name of Jack Saul. Jack Saul was a real person, as were other characters in the book, including Stella and Fanny, aka Ernest Boulton and Frederick Park. There are some real locations such as hotels and restaurants. But *The Sins of the Cities of the Plain* is almost entirely fiction or, rather, pornographic fiction. It was clearly written by someone, or more than one, who knew the queer culture of nineteenth-century London very well indeed. The narrator alluded to a tobacconist's shop next door to the Albany Barracks in Regent's Park where willing guardsmen might be found, and revealed that there were six other brothels in London 'where only soldiers are received and where gentlemen can sleep with them'.

One of the authors of *The Sins of the Cities of the Plain* has been suggested to be Simeon Solomon, an artist whose social and cultural career came to an end after he had been found having sex with an old man in a public lavatory; he was fined the very large sum of one hundred pounds. Eventually he was admitted to St Giles's Workhouse. It may be that the book was in part his revenge against the polite hypocrisies of society. 'Jack Saul', for example, reveals that 'the extent to which pederasty is carried on in London between gentlemen and young fellows is little dreamed of by the outside public'. Small fragments of reported conversation also have the ring of authenticity. 'I see you are evidently a fast young chap . . . ready for a lark with a free gentleman at any time . . . Did you ever see such a fine tosser [cock] in your life . . .' It has the unmistakable flavour of the period, as does the standard overture of both male and female prostitutes to a likely client. 'Are you good-natured, sir?'

This is the context for one of the most badly conceived interventions into sexual practices that was ever perpetrated by Parliament. In 1885 the Criminal Law Amendment Act was being debated in the Commons when one Liberal MP, Henry Labouchere, proposed an amendment to the effect that 'any male person who, in public, or private, commits, or is a party to the commission of, or procures, or attempts to procure the commission by any male person of any act of gross indecency with another male person, shall be guilty of a misdemeanour and being convicted thereof shall be liable at the discretion of the court to be imprisoned for any term not exceeding two years with or without hard labour'.

It was a judgement more harsh than any previously imposed. There was no attempt to prove sexual penetration or emission as a mark of crime. There was no distinction between private and public acts. There was no attempt to define what was meant by 'gross indecency'. The studied vagueness and ambiguity of the amendment rendered it a charter for any blackmailer or ill-disposed person to level a charge against another man without any need for positive evidence or even for a witness. Mutual masturbation, for example, was rendered illegal and subject to a jail term. It says something about the nature of English justice that the amendment remained on the statute book until 1967. It has been said in defence of Labouchere that he introduced the clause as a 'wrecking amendment' to force re-examination of the entire bill; but all it managed to wreck were the lives of queer men.

One subsequent real-life court dialogue of 1889 might have come straight from *The Sins of the Cities of the Plain*.

'Where did you meet this person?'

'In Piccadilly, between Albany courtyard and Sackville Street. He laughed at me and I winked at him. He turned sharp into Sackville Street . . . the Duke, as we called him, came near me and asked me where I was going. I said "home", and he said, "what sort is your place?" "Very comfortable" I replied. He said, "is it very quiet there?" I said yes, it was, and we took a hansom cab there. We got out by the Middlesex Hospital, and I took

> the gentleman to 19 Cleveland Street, letting him in with my latchkey.'

The witness was none other than Jack Saul, the young male prostitute whose haphazard memories had been taken up by the author or authors of *The Sins of the Cities of the Plain*. He was as real as any costermonger. The 'gentleman' in question was Lord Euston, and he had become embroiled in what was soon known as the 'Cleveland Street Scandal'.

It had begun with the unexpected affluence of some telegraph boys from the General Post Office. Telegraph boys were popular in certain circles and one man, accused of sodomy in 1877, stated that 'the crime for which I am sentenced has been very prevalent amongst the Telegraph lads . . . many have been found out and dismissed in consequence'. The 'lads' were a regular turn. They arrived on the doorstep with the telegraph message. They were quick, lively and, as cockneys, knew all the ways of London. They dealt with ready money from their clients wishing for the urgent news. They were smart in the bottom-hugging uniforms.

Some verses of the period were entitled *Love in Earnest* (1892). 'Earnest' was a slang word for queer, as, perhaps, in Oscar Wilde's *The Importance of Being Earnest*.

> Smart-looking boys are in my line;
> The lad that gives my boots a shine,
> The lad that works the lift below,
> The lad that's lettered G.P.O.

The G.P.O. lads were perfect for the man who wanted a boy without having to hunt the streets for him. These 'modern Mercuries' could also be male whores.

And so it had proved in the spring of 1884 when a young telegraph boy, Thomas Swinscow, was found to be carrying eighteen shillings of the coin of the realm. He was of course suspected of theft but when questioned he replied after some hesitation that he had received the shillings from a Mr Hammond and that 'I got the money from going to bed with gentlemen at his house' in Cleveland Street. Cleveland Street, a nondescript throughfare close to Tottenham Court Road, could have been made for surreptitious sex. Other telegraph boys were associated with the same address, and in the process they named several important clients including Lord Euston and Lord Arthur Somerset who managed the stables of the Prince of Wales. Prince Eddy, the name familiarly given to the son of the Prince of Wales, was also subject to whispers and rumours.

It had to come out in the end. A journalist from the radical *North London Press* named names. Lord Somerset, Lord Euston and others had attended a male brothel at 19 Cleveland Street, where there seem to have been more telegraph boys than in the General Post Office. Some of the evidence, from the notorious Jack Saul in particular, was interesting.

> 'And were you hunted by the police?'
>
> 'No. They have never interfered. They have always been kind to me.'
>
> 'Do you mean that they have deliberately shut their eyes to your infamous practices?'
>
> 'They have had to shut their eyes to more than me.'

Saul, despite declaring that he was a 'professional Maryanne', admitted that he earned his living in part by house-cleaning for female prostitutes. There was a solidarity in the suffering sisterhood.

In the face of vague or inconsistent testimony from the prosecution witnesses, the case against the Cleveland Street queers fell to pieces. Somerset had been spirited out of the country, while Prince Eddy began a tour of India. A determined opponent of the English legal system might find here some evidence of conspiracy, but even at this late date nothing can be definitively proved. The suspicion lingers, however, that the more eminent the defendant, the easier it was to slip the bounds of justice. As one young telegraph boy put it, 'I think it very hard that I should get into trouble while men in high position are allowed to walk about free.' This, however, is the condition of queer London.

A NIGHT IN THE CAVE OF THE GOLDEN CALF.

17

Damned and done for

Oscar Wilde was subjected to three trials, one for libel in which he was the instigator and two for gross indecency in which he was the accused. He foolishly miscalculated by pursuing the Marquess of Queensberry for accusing him of 'posing as a somdomite'; it was not wise to appeal to the English legal system in the guise of a victim. Wilde's ill-advised libel action gave an additional legitimacy to the whole process of pursuing and punishing queers.

Wilde knew that Queensberry had what in the language of card players and gamblers is called a trump card. Queensberry's eldest son, Viscount Drumlanrig, was suspected of having a queer affair with Lord Rosebery who became prime minister in 1894. Drumlanrig had been his private secretary. Drumlanrig had committed suicide seven months after his employer became premier, but Queensberry is supposed to have had in his possession a compromising letter between the two men. It would have provoked a political sensation and it is possible that Queensberry threatened to make public Rosebery's predilections if the administration did not pursue Wilde to the uttermost. Since Wilde had taken up with one of Queensberry's other sons, Lord Alfred Douglas, here would have been poetic as well as legal justice. In the libel trial, after a more than usually intimate cross-examination of Wilde, Queensberry was acquitted.

The second trial also did not proceed as planned. Queensberry and his detectives had trawled the streets of London for likely young catches, willing to accuse Wilde of sodomy and other unnatural practices, but the jury was not entirely convinced. At this second trial Wilde was asked to define 'the love that dare not speak its name'. He responded in his most golden tones, invoking Plato and Shakespeare, Michelangelo and David. 'It is the deep spiritual affection that is as pure as it is perfect . . . It is beautiful, it is fine, it is the noblest form of expression . . . The world mocks at it and sometimes puts one in the pillory for it.' It remains one of the most impassioned defences of queerness since Plato's *Symposium*, and may have helped to save him momentarily from ruin. The jury could not reach a verdict. Wilde left the Old Bailey and fled for refuge to his mother and brother in Oakley Street. 'Willie, give me shelter,' he is supposed to have called out to his brother, 'or I shall die in the streets.'

The jury at the third trial, which followed soon after, had not the advantage of hearing Wilde's eloquent apologia, and had no doubt about the writer's guilt on eight out of nine counts of indecency. His crimes were compounded by his evident delight in boys of a lower class. Shakespeare and Michelangelo counted less than the physical proofs of the buggery of young men. As a result of these trials, certain facts of queer life became known to the general public, from the stains on the bed sheets of respectable hotels to the private rooms of restaurants where men and boys might exchange kisses or more.

One of Wilde's acquaintances, Alfred Taylor, had chambers that might have come out of a French novel. 'The windows of his rooms,' his landlady remarked at the second trial, 'were covered with stained art muslin and dark curtains and lace curtains. They were furnished sumptuously, and were lighted by different coloured lamps and candles . . . The windows were never opened and the daylight was never admitted.' If it were necessary to venture outside, the restaurants of choice were the Café Royal, Kettners, the Florence, the St James's and Solferino's. These were the temples, or at least the anterooms, of queer London.

It has become customary to canonise, or at least to beatify, Wilde. He claimed later that his decisions were the only proper ones since 'To regret one's own experiences is to arrest one's own development. To deny one's own experiences is to put a lie into the lips of one's own life. It is no less than a denial of the soul.' With this defiance he earned his place with the very highest of those who have defended themselves in the dock. But it did not seem so at the time. He was for a while a byword for sexual infamy. On the night of his conviction it was said that six hundred English gentlemen crossed the Channel, and well into the twentieth century any apparent homosexual was greeted with catcalls of 'Oscar! Oscar!' He had always denied conventional reality but now he and others were impaled upon it. He had once explained that an interpretation was more suggestive than a fact but now he was destroyed by the interpretations of others. The *Echo* rejoiced that he was 'damned and done for'.

Wilde returned to the Old Bailey for sentencing, and the judge consigned him to the full Labouchere punishment of two years with hard labour. 'My God, my God,' he called out. 'And I? May I say nothing, my lord?' The judge waved him away, and he was carried in a closed van to Newgate, from which he was removed along a via dolorosa to Holloway and then to Pentonville.

The publicity granted to Wilde's trial and to the Cleveland Street affair concentrated public attention on London as the nursery of vice. The front pages of *Reynold's News* had successive headlines, 'OTHER SERIOUS CHARGES' and 'OTHER CASES – HORRIBLE CONDITION OF LONDON'. The members of the press were on the watch, further aroused by the mass-circulation newspapers that specialised in scandal and sensation. Five court cases repeated the Wildean experience of an older man seducing a younger boy. A chemist's assistant, John Goodchild, for example, was convicted for luring a Jewish match-seller into 'acts of gross indecency'. Walter Woolverton, a well-known and highly respectable member of the YMCA, was arrested for committing gross indecency in a boat-race crowd. Was nowhere safe? A public urinal off Oxford Street also came to the attention of journalists.

Some urinals had a worldwide reputation. 'Clarkson's Cottage' was known for its proximity to Willie Clarkson's theatrical costume shop and it was purchased after the Second World War by a rich American who erected it, in memory of happy days, within the grounds of his New York estate. The toilets in Down Street underground station, off Piccadilly, were deservedly popular. It was reported that 'urinals have a certain odour . . . a staleness [which] . . . excites [queer men] as if they were so many dogs on heat'. Another favourite was a three-stall urinal down a flight of steps beside the Yorkshire Stingo on the Marylebone Road. The toilet beside the Lyric Theatre in Hammersmith was 'chock a block from dusk to dawn'. Some preferred of course the relative warmth of the theatres themselves, especially in the rear areas labelled 'standing room only'. One theatregoer standing at the back of the Islington Music Hall noted that 'someone undone my flies and started pulling me out . . . while they were doing it someone pushed themselves up against me expecting me to do it to them'. 'It was no uncommon sight,' a contemporary remarked, 'to see literally hundreds of young men . . . walking about, talking in high-pitched voices, recognizing one another.'

In *A Problem in Modern Ethics* (1896) John Addington Symonds, who has already wandered into this study, suggested that in London 'inverted sexuality runs riot', and he named various 'rioters' including men to be found 'in drawing-rooms, law-courts, banks, universities, mess-rooms on the bench, the throne, the chair of the professor, under the blouse of the workman, the cassock of the priest, the epaulettes of the officer, the smock-frock of the ploughman, the wig of the barrister, the mantle of the peer, the costume of the actor, the tights of the athlete, the gown of the academician'. It is a colourful list, but what was 'the throne' doing there?

In the following year George Ives, part of the queer world of the period, founded the Order of the Chaeronea, a secret society of men who favoured 'the Hellenistic ideal', which presumably included love between men and boys. It represented a 'common cause' of mutual duty and self-sacrifice, although these virtues were not outstanding in 1897. The order was supposed to represent an idealised community along the lines of the Sacred Band of Thebes, lovers who fought together in battle, unfortunately massacred by Philip II of Macedon at the Battle of Chaeronea in 338 BC. This did not provide an apt precedent, perhaps, and the Order of the Chaeronea hardly got beyond the realm of good intentions. The class of Greek translation at Cambridge in 1910, according to E. M. Forster's *Maurice* (not published until after the author's death), was cautioned that it was necessary to 'omit a reference to the unspeakable vice of the Greeks'.

Ives's small band of brothers, which included Edward Carpenter, celebrated same-sex love as part of a masculine ideal of egalitarian partnership that somehow transcended class-based behaviour. They were full of good intentions but seemed ultimately preposterous in their excursions to the gymnasia, the public swimming baths and the nude bathing sections of the Serpentine. 'Early in the morning,' Symonds wrote, 'I used to rise from a sleepless bed, walk across the park, and feed my eyes on the naked men and boys bathing in the Serpentine.' Even though he was perhaps inspired by the highest possible motives, others might have seen him as a seedy voyeur. He also proposed the notion that certain areas of the public parks should be reserved for queer men and be known as 'spoonitoria', from the word for cuddling from behind.

Like much of Symonds, this suggestion may seem a little hypothetical and old-fashioned. The law, however, was not necessarily sympathetic. In 1898 the Vagrancy Law Amendment Act was passed; it was intended to prosecute men 'who in any public place persistently solicit or importune for immoral purposes'. The actual nature of the offence was not named. A smile, a nod, a wink or a whistle might be the occasion for prosecution.

A correspondent of Havelock Ellis, whose testimony is printed in Ellis's *Studies in the Psychology of Sex* (1897–1928), noted that 'with regard to the general inability of inverts to whistle, their fondness for green, their feminine calligraphy, skill at female occupations etc., these all seem to be but indications of the one principle. To go still further and include trivial things, few inverts even smoke in the same manner and with the same enjoyment as a man; they have seldom the male facility at games, cannot throw at a mark with precision or even spit!' They were supposed to have longer fingers. It was also said that queer men wore patent leather shoes, and that they preferred to wear their overcoats over their shoulders. At a later date the 'look' had turned to suede shoes, Liberty ties and camel-hair coats. The 1890s was the decade when queerness became an object of scientific as well as medical awareness. It had always been a matter of absorbing interest since the days of antiquity but in the work of Ellis, Krafft-Ebing and others it became a psychological as well as a physiological condition.

Men were not necessarily the centre of unusual sexual attention. Lord Alfred Douglas, the inciter and abettor of Oscar Wilde, wrote a letter to the *Review of Reviews* in order to point out that 'perhaps you are not aware that "lesbianism" exists to any extent in London, but I can assure you that it does, and though of course I cannot mention names, I could point out to you half a dozen women in society or among actresses who would be considered as "dangerous" to young girls as Oscar Wilde will I suppose henceforth be considered to boys'. The letter was not published.

In fact women were as much the object of scientific or psychological enquiry as men. Havelock Ellis and John Addington Symonds worked together on a volume entitled *Sexual Inversion* (1897) in which they stated that 'it is usually considered as no offence at all in women. Another reason is that it is less easy to detect in women, we are accustomed to much greater familiarity in intimacy between women than between men, and we are less apt to suspect the existence of an abnormal passion. A woman may feel a high degree of sexual attraction for another woman, without realizing that her affection is sexual . . .'

Ellis was a little more open in the first volume of his *Studies in the Psychology of Sex* where he stated that 'passionate friendships among girls, from the most innocent to the most elaborate excursions in the direction of Lesbos, are extremely common in theatres, both among actresses and, even more, among chorus and ballet girls. Here the pell-mell of the dressing rooms, the wait of perhaps two hours between the performances, during which all the girls are cooped up, in a state of inaction and excitement, in a few crowded dressing-rooms afford every opportunity for the growth of this particular kind of sentiment.'

At a slightly later date, in 1901, Ellis went further. 'A Catholic confessor, a friend tells me, informed him that for one man who acknowledges homosexual practices, there are three women.' He even diverged into physical detail. 'Homosexual passion in women finds more or less complete expression in kissing, sleeping together and close embrace, as in what is sometimes called "lying spoons".' Sigmund Freud believed that bisexuality 'comes to the fore much more clearly in women than in men'; unlike men they had two sexual organs, the vagina or female organ and the clitoris 'which is analogous to the male organ'.

A foreign noblewoman, known only as Countess V—, who had lived in London for some years, killed herself in 1901. Another self-professed expert on queer living, Xavier Mayne, described her case in *The Intersexes* (1910): 'she was also robust to virility, though not amazonian or coarse. She had been allowed in childhood an almost boyish liberty of tastes, amusements, dress and so on. She was a hunter of large game and an expert boxer and fencer . . .'

Catherine Coome in the same period earned her living first as a painter and decorator on P&O steamers before becoming a highly respected decorator in the West End. She had then 'married' the female servant in the family of Lady Campbell at Hampton Court. At her subsequent trial for fraud it was reported that 'the prisoner looked thoroughly masculine, and the voice and manner were so man-like that there was no wonder in her identity being unguessed'. The 'wife' of Catherine Coome 'had never suspected' that her spouse was not a man.

A similar situation emerged in London in 1912 when two young women shared an interest in Christian social work among the poor. It was one of those causes that late-Victorian and Edwardian women took up with enthusiasm. They began to live as man and wife. The 'husband' earned a living as a plumber's mate, and became renowned for his skill at 'fisticuffs' in the mission halls and elsewhere. He was at last discovered by his partner's brother in circumstances that are not entirely clear. This story had for once a happy ending. The law was mild with the two women and 'as they remained devoted to each other, arrangements were made for them to live together'. Another young woman was continually arrested for wearing male clothes. When asked what would break the habit, she replied 'if I could go to sea', no doubt on the principle that all the nice girls love a sailor.

Some did not need to hide. In 1912 Madame Strindberg opened a basement club in Heddon Street, just off Regent Street, and therefore in the centre of gay London to which couples of both sexes flocked. It was called the Cave of the Golden Calf, which seemed to promise almost biblical licentiousness. It had been decorated by Wyndham Lewis, Eric Gill and Jacob Epstein, and so might just pass muster as an artistic establishment; but it is doubtful if anyone was fooled.

It could not have been further, socially and artistically, from the painted boys of a rendezvous along the Edgware Road identified by one urban wanderer, Thomas Burke, who stated that 'you may know these places by the strong odour of scent when you enter them, and the absence of women. The sweet boys stand at the counter . . . under the wandering eyes of middle aged grey faced men.' It was not an alluring prospect. Some queers were past caring. The Marquess of Anglesey, heavily perfumed and beringed, walked his pink-ribboned poodle through the streets of Mayfair. It was an egregious example of title, and wealth, triumphing over the force of public opinion. The birch, brought back in 1911 for homosexual offences, was reserved for those who were considered to be of lower-middle-class origin or worse.

A measure of the dismay that queerness still aroused in the upper-middle class is revealed in E. M. Forster's *Maurice* when the eponymous hero is told by another young man, 'I love you.' 'Maurice was scandalized, horrified . . . "Oh rot! . . . Durham, you're an Englishman. I'm another. Don't talk nonsense . . . it's the only subject absolutely beyond the limit . . ."' Durham admits that 'most men would have reported me to the Dean or the Police'. A brief conversation from the novel may be admitted as further evidence of repression.

> 'I say, in your rounds here, do you come across unspeakables of the Oscar Wilde sort?'
>
> 'No, that's in the asylum work, thank God.'

Fact was no less menacing than fiction. In 1912 an actor, Alan Horton, was imprisoned for two weeks simply for walking into a urinal 'with a wiggle'. In Compton Mackenzie's novel of the following year, *Sinister Street*, a young man is approached by what might be called an aesthete. 'Won't you smoke? These Chian cigarettes in their diaphanous paper of mildest mauve would suit your oddly remote, your curiously shy glance . . .'

Xavier Mayne pasted into his notebook a newspaper clipping concerning a servant who had been arrested on the Euston Road: 'He wore an irreproachably fitting black walking costume of the newest fashion, made to order, a grey feather boa, and a coquettish hat of fine net . . . He resented the arrest, in great indignation, declaring to the officer, "you wretch! I am a lady!" As the officer did not regard this statement, the complainant gave him a violent blow in the face and a fierce battle began at once, in which the "lady" bit the officer's finger. Only with the assistance of three other policemen could he be overpowered and brought, struggling, biting, scratching and spitting, to the police station.'

The First World War was, for most queers of either sex, a welcome opportunity. Women in uniform were no longer considered as 'mannish' but as patriots; close-cropped hair and working boots were becoming indispensable in difficult work. And why not roll your own cigarettes? All the men did. The dockyards, factories and arsenals were soon filled with women workers, while public transport came to depend on their efforts. One million women, or more, became recruits in what had once been a masculine world and the sexual balance in every respect began to change. Natural homoerotic tendencies, once repressed in the line of domestic duty, were released. Women became 'mates', in ways that had not previously been possible. Naomi, known as 'Micky', ran a munitions factory in Willesden. Lillian Barker was superintendent of Woolwich Arsenal while living with her girlfriend.

The laws of demand and supply catered for the influx of soldiers into the city. New gay clubs, bars and pubs were established – the Empire, the Trocadero, the Wellington and the Griffin among them. Lyons' Corner House in Coventry Street became known as the Lillypond. In the face of death and destruction, an instinct for self-expression, or liberation, became visible.

It was said that some soldiers unbuttoned their flies on the way to disembarkation. The 'blackout' was like a transformation scene in a pantomime. The familiar world went into hiding. Certain theatres, including the Prince of Wales, were known for their policy of 'anything goes'. Robert Hutton wrote that 'when dusk fell a feeling of restlessness and excitement crept over me'. Some bars bowed to demand by catering for two different types of clientele. Heterosexual couples would rub shoulders, if nothing else, with young men who wore lipstick and mascara. The Long Bar at the Trocadero and the Circle Bar at the Palladium were nominal rivals but they shared their clients in happy bonhomie; there was the Tea Kettle in Wardour Street and the Chalice Bar sometimes known as the Poisoned Chalice. A basement club in Endell Street, the Caravan, was advertised as 'London's Greatest Bohemian Rendezvous'. But the Criterion, in Piccadilly, probably merited that status; sailors entering down the wide staircase were greeted with applause. So many were summoned and all were chosen. The Running Horse, known as 'The Mare', was one of the most celebrated of evening rendezvous. It might have been believed by visitors that the streets of London were paved with men rather than with gold. Some old regulars, such as the Rockingham, the 'A&B', the Spartan, and the Festival, survived into the sixties and even into the seventies.

Many clubs for women were known and named. The Cave of Harmony, the Orange Tree and the Hambone were believed to harbour women with short-cropped hair, women with monocles and women with little green cigars.

It was rumoured during the First World War that the Germans had compiled a black book of prominent English queers, of both sexes, who might be blackmailed after a German victory. Noel Pemberton Billing, a former pilot and editor of the *Imperialist*, wrote an article in which he claimed that the Berlin Black Book contained the names of 47,000 'highly placed British perverts' who were trained to undermine the male youth of the country. In a further publication, *Vigilante*, he claimed in an article entitled 'The Cult of the Clitoris' that an actress named Maud Allan was a lesbian co-conspirator. Allan sued but lost her case. The jury seemed to regard Pemberton Billing in the light of a national hero.

It might be considered that lesbianism was as threatening as the enemy and even tantamount to treason. In a debate on the Criminal Law Amendment Bill in 1921, one MP, Frederick Macquisten, proposed a clause rendering any act of gross indecency between women a criminal offence. He affirmed that 'there is in modern social life an undercurrent of dreadful degradation, unchecked and uninterfered with'. Only that night, he added, he had commiserated with a friend 'who told him how his home had been ruined by the wiles of one abandoned female who had pursued his wife'. A judge, Sir Ernest Wild, mentioned that not a week passed 'but some unfortunate girl does not confess to him that she owes the breakdown of her nerves to the fact that she had been tampered with by a member of her own sex'. From the evidence of these eminent men it would appear that lesbianism had reached epidemic proportions after the close of the First World War. It is clear that many women – some of whom had done the jobs of men and some of whom had escaped from domestic service in the home, and had worked in factories, on farms and even the docks – felt horribly 'put back in the box' when the men came home from the Front.

A book of lesbian love provoked outrage in 1928. *The Well of Loneliness* by Radclyffe Hall purported to be the story of an altogether mannish female, Stephen Gordon, who eventually finds solace with a female companion. The text by no stretch of the imagination could be described as pornographic, or even mildly titillating, but the chief magistrate at Bow Court nevertheless deemed it to be an 'obscene libel'. The Director of Public Prosecutions upheld that judgement when he declared that 'a large amount of curiosity has been excited among women and I am afraid in many cases curiosity may lead to imagination and indulgence in practices'. There was a great deal of fuss over one remark in particular: 'she kissed her full on the lips, like a lover'. Radclyffe Hall explained at the time that 'I wrote the book from a deep sense of duty. I am proud indeed to have taken up my pen in defence of those who are utterly defenceless.' A reviewer in the *Sunday Express* felt obliged to disagree. 'I would rather put a phial of prussic acid in the hands of a healthy girl or boy than the book in question.' The book was withdrawn. Hall herself was of distinctively masculine appearance, complete with pipe and monocle; as a person, rather than as a writer, she was accepted as the embodiment of the thoroughly English eccentric.

The case against *The Well of Loneliness* did more to fashion the identity of the female queer than any other trial or scandal of the period; in certain respects it proclaimed the birth of the lesbian in the twentieth century, complete with shingled hair, tailored suits, stiff collars and flannelled shirts together with low-heeled patent leather shoes. It was the annunciation of what was called at the time 'the third sex' or, more flippantly, 'the Boyette'. 'She had never been quite like the other children,' Stephen Gordon recalls, 'she had always been lonely and discontented.' That was the central text of *The Well of Loneliness* which convinced its readers. I have always been lonely. I will always stand outside the world. I know it. For many queers, male or female, life was a vale of tears.

*

It is arguable that in the first half of the twentieth century, however, gays of both sexes were subject to a level of prejudice and intolerance not seen before in Western history; entrapment, imprisonment and sudden police raids became familiar characteristics of London life. All this was to change in the last decades of the century, but nobody knew that at the time. Until the sixties and early seventies it was the same grey and furtive atmosphere of surveillance and arrests. In 1939 a reporter from the *People* noted of the bars for either sex 'that they flourish by the score in dingy side-streets, alley-ways, cellars and basements between Oxford Street and Charing Cross . . . The surroundings are always the same – they keep the lights low to hide the dirty walls . . . and a handful of semi-drunks going through the motions of dancing on a tiny patch of linoleum.' One was arrested for wearing 'rouge and had a powder puff in his pocket'. A principal target had become now the ubiquitous 'bedsits', close enough to the city centres, where passion flourished in small anonymous rooms. 'Well, I don't mind the beastly raid,' one of the victims is alleged to have said, 'but I would like to know if you can let me have one of your nice boys to come home with me. I am really good.' This may have been one of those 'gay' repartees which made queerness less serious and less threatening.

But the public lavatories were still at the top of the list for furtive encounters. They were sometimes known as 'tin chapels', as if sacred rituals were conducted within. One client might be informally chosen as 'watch-out' for the visiting stranger or policeman. The urinals around the back of Jermyn Street were well known to the acting profession, and the public lavatory at Waterloo Station was positively cornucopian. The toilet at Hill Place was a magnet for 'toffs' or anyone in evening dress.

One contemporary recorded that 'these small unobtrusive

urinals were in many areas, the most important places for homosexuals of all and every kind. Always open, usually unattended, and consisting of a small number of stalls, over the sides of which it was quite easy to spy and get a sight of one's neighbour's cock, they were ideally built for the gratification of the voyeur's sexual itch.' The activity or practice was known as 'cottaging', no doubt named after the plain single-storey toilets that in part resembled the simplest cottages in Arcadia. Their narrow and malodorous compartments were full of drawings and caricatures of a phallic nature, together with pornographic graffiti and requests for carnal meetings at a certain time and on a certain date. It is not clear how many of these were taken up. But the walls were a life class for sex.

A pseudonymous account of the urinary situation, *For Your Convenience: A Learned Dialogue Instructive to all Londoners and London Visitors, Overheard at the Thélème Club and Taken Down Verbatim*, was published in 1937. It was supposed to have been written by the succinctly named Paul Pry but was in fact the work of Thomas Burke whom the reader last encountered in the purlieus of the Edgware Road. Under the guise of a sanitary expert, 'Paul Pry' investigates the most prominent lavatories of London in the company of a chirpy young man who takes on the guiding role of Dante's Virgil in the 'Inferno'.

The young man, however, does not speak in terza rima. 'In a cul-de-sac at the end of that passage you would have found full service, with bright railings round it. And in a street on the right, just below Marylebone Lane and going towards Portman Square – in that street is a public yard provided with one of those zinc or iron enclosures painted a grateful green . . . You see, places of that kind which have no attendants afford excellent rendezvous to people who wish to meet out of doors and yet escape the eye of the Busy.' The young man mentions crooks and bookies as possible beneficiaries of his advice, but his real audience is clear. 'When, for instance, I have been at a loss in Dalston, in Streatham, in Clerkenwell, in Bermondsey, knowledge acquired on previous journeys has always been a blessing.' He takes all London as his province. 'In the section between Oxford Circus and Tottenham Court Road, places may be found at the bottom of Argyll Street.' Chancery Lane might seem to be a wilderness except for 'the little turning opposite Bream's Buildings'. Onc of thc most fruitful ncighbourhoods is that part of south London by the bridges, and in particular Borough High Street. Vegetable markets are always popular, as is St Paul's, Covent Garden.

His route became a pilgrimage for those who could avoid the policeman or the ruffian, but for others not so fortunate it became a broadway to perdition. If you were arrested, taken up and taken away, your family, your employment, your prospects were gone in an instant. One man wrote to a Member of Parliament at a time of debate on the question that 'it is all right for people to condemn us so much but they have no idea of the life of fear and dread we live all the time, in case our friends find out or we are caught. I know I did, and I know the hell I lived in when the police came to me, and I'm still living in hell now!' There was also of course the ever-present danger of blackmail. Those who could afford it preferred exile; others made do with the silence of fear and trembling. Two men, found guilty of sex in a taxi, flung themselves into the icy Thames to find their quietus.

london 1971

10p

gay liberation front manifesto

18

Howl

When the lights went out, during the Second World War, a strange mood compounded of fear, hysteria and excitement affected the people of London. Everything was turned upside down, including once more the role and status of the sexes. Any particular sexual orientation was of lesser interest in a world where you might be killed or injured at any moment. Those who have watched the domestic films of the forties may recall that the voices of the women carry more weight than those of the men – whether it be on the factory floor, in the bomb shelter or in the kitchen.

A genuine confraternity existed in the streets and public spaces of London, and it was not unusual to find soldiers and seamen frequenting public houses, particularly those in the East End, which would remain open all night for whatever purposes were deemed necessary. The added vein of darkness during the blackouts increased the sexual tensions of a world where everything seemed permissible. As Quentin Crisp put it, 'never in the history of sex was so much offered by so many to so few'. It is often quoted as 'to so many by so few'. It can be taken either way without distortion. In any case it did not last long after the lights were lifted.

As a form of official retribution, perhaps, the immediate post-war years were dominated by fear and suspicion. Nightclubs as furtive as their clientele, public houses that somehow survived by bribery of the police, 'cottaging' in always dangerous situations, clandestine street encounters were the order of the night. The campaign by the upholders of the law against queers was in fact intensified in the fifties. Ever more sensational and salacious cases were publicised by the ever-devouring press. Those affairs have now been forgotten but at the time they were the subject of front-page headlines. It is not too much to confirm that the police, and the newspapers, were then the objects of terror among gay people. Letters and photograph albums were burned in case of incriminatory suspicions. Men who were visited by the police often fled their immediate neighbourhood. Suicide may have occurred in numbers larger than reported.

Eight policemen, in groups of two, monitored the public lavatories in a well-worn circuit from Victoria Station to Bloomsbury Way. The level of arrests increased exponentially, as did the incidence of blackmail. Some men were given immunity from persecution if they testified against others. All of them were, according to one prosecuting barrister, 'perverts, men of the lowest character'. Other expressions of disgust were common. It would not be too much to say that an incipient police state was beginning to emerge, assisted by the various home secretaries, directors of public prosecution and assorted judges and magistrates.

Numerous well-publicised cases sustained prurient attention among the readers of newspapers. A group of young guardsmen were caught 'riding around in a harness' for the benefit of their customers at a flat in Curzon Street, Mayfair. The activities of the customers in the Fitzroy Tavern also became the subject of a court case. A student of this history might be forgiven for thinking that she or he has read it all before. It is part of the London story.

In the fifties the deities of family, home and marriage were all the more venerated after the destruction of the previous decade; they were also the triune figures of the new welfare state. Half of eligible men were married in 1921, three-quarters of them in 1951. The public state was closing ranks, and there emerged once more what was known as 'the threat of homosexuality'.

It was in the context of quiet and not so quiet persecution that the Wolfenden Committee was established in 1954 to inquire into the legal status of homosexual acts. The committee comprised the great and the good, but they were neither conventionally 'liberal' nor unprudish in their social attitudes. For the sake of the ladies present at the proceedings, homosexuals were known as Huntleys and prostitutes as Palmers after a well-known firm of biscuit makers.

Its report, published in 1957, recommended that 'homosexual behaviour between consenting adults in private should no longer be a criminal offence'. It was followed in 1958 by the establishment of the Homosexual Law Reform Society to support 'those suffering from intolerance, persecution and social injustice'. This was complemented by such studies as Michael Schofield's *A Minority: A Report on the Life of the Male Homosexual in Great Britain*, published in 1960, in which the author suggested that 'the homosexual must be studied in the wide context of the whole community'.

But the Wolfenden recommendations were not passed into law as the Sexual Offences Act until 1967; the new Act followed the Labouchere Amendment of 1885, and so for more than eighty years the Victorian edict had remained in force. The paradoxical result was that, by the time the new Act had passed, many queer people had lost interest in the technical provisions of the law. Such provisions already seemed irrelevant and even farcical. The reports and observations of the Wolfenden

Committee may have brought much needed light and air to a pursuit that had been shrouded in darkness and mystery. Yet it made very little difference to queers themselves. The lifting of certain regulations seemed to have no effect upon magistrates and policemen who simply redoubled their efforts. Criminal convictions rose in the years following the acceptance of the recommendations of 1957.

It has been suggested that in the 1960s London became in many respects a sexually liberated space. It did not seem like that at the time. In the early part of the decade – before the Sexual Offences Act of 1967 – it was still cloistered and claustrophobic, a city where queerness was discussed in low voices and where police activity was still eminently visible. In September 1960 E. M. Forster wrote in an epilogue to his novel of 1914, *Maurice*, that 'we had not realised that what the public truly loathes in homosexuality is not the thing itself but having to think about it'. He turned out to be spectacularly wrong. But the furtive nature of the time may have contributed to his nervousness. Few came out yelling and screaming in support of a more liberal attitude to homosexuals in England, although Allen Ginsberg's 'Howl' of 1955 helped the process in the United States. Someone, somewhere, may have been 'swinging' in Queer City but the general mood among homosexuals was still one of discretion and subdued gaiety. The playwright Joe Orton was the Rimbaud of what he called 'pissoirs'; in his diary of 1967, there are references to 'the trade' and to a variety of 'queens'. Sex seems to have been readily available, but treated in a haphazard and rather pointless manner. The lacklustre atmosphere may well be a testament to the real rather than the mythic conditions of London in the sixties.

Places of assignation were as well frequented as ever, but the new arrivals in London had some difficulty in finding them.

A little club in High Street Kensington, a little pub in Hampstead were slim pickings. Soho and Earls Court raised the temperature, but London was lukewarm and always vulnerable to the attentions of what was known as 'Lillie Law'.

'Lillie Law' knew all the old haunts. The White Bear, beneath the 'circus' of Piccadilly, was one of the survivors. The Criterion, close by and happily above ground, attracted its regular clientele by ten in the evening. In case of customer fatigue, the Standard and Ward's Irish Bar were in the immediate neighbourhood. To the north of Oxford Street stood the Bricklayers Arms, the Fitzroy Tavern, the Wheatsheaf and the Marquess of Granby. Le Gigolo, in the King's Road, was the favourite of those who liked to wilt in a crush of men. The Kandy Lounge and the Pink Elephant and the A&B were all in Soho, while the public houses there were joined by coffee bars, among them the Haymarket Coffee House and the Matelot in Panton Street. The geographical dispersal of coffee bars in Soho was the harbinger for the gay occupation of that neighbourhood in later decades. The map of London could in fact be marked by myriad scarlet stars as signs of occupation, but the venues remained for the most part unknown to name and fame except by those who frequented them.

One of the most famous venues in the city in the 1960s was like some remnant of an earlier age; the Biograph, known colloquially as the Bio-Grope, was close to Victoria Station and must have been one of the few cinemas where no one came to see the film. Instead it was filled with the creaking of old seats as one or another customer moved from one row to the next in search of more obvious fun.

Among women, according to queer memoirs of the period, the process of meeting a partner was often hesitant and diffident . . .

somebody knew somebody who knew somebody. The entrance to a new world was not always easy. Women seem to have avoided the promiscuity that males practised in toilet and street. There were one or two nightclubs that catered for queer women, such as the Fiesta in Notting Hill Gate, but some novices or adventurers were nonplussed by a rigid sexual coding which had developed and which divided girls into 'butch' or 'femme'. You had to pass as one or other, complete with Brylcreemed hair for the former and handbags for the latter, or you were deemed to possess no sexual identity at all. The butch wore shirt and tie; the femme wore skirt and blouse. For some women this was as depressing as the sexual stereotyping of the heterosexual world, but it was perhaps an inevitable aspect of this age of transition.

The most famous of all venues for queer women was a club on the corner of Bramerton Street and the King's Road. Like many semi-mythical phenomena, the true origins of Gateways are still in doubt. Throughout the 1940s and 50s it had a mixed clientele, male and female, comprising mainly those who did not quite fit the starched atmosphere of the period. It came into its own as a gay haunt for women in the 1960s, and did not close until 1985. Once again, however, sheltering behind an anonymous green door, it bore the marks of secrecy and isolation. Gay women had not yet emerged in the office or in the shop; they were at ease only behind closed doors.

Social change, prompted by the unknown laws of life, is inevitable. The Gay Liberation Front (or GLF, as it came to be known) marked what seemed to many to be the first assertion of gay identity without apology or equivocation. The meetings were as likely to be made up of hippies as white-collar workers, of students as well as teachers. It represented, therefore, the single most vocal sexual opposition to what soon became known (at least among many queers) as 'straight' culture. Straight culture was the culture of the suits, of the politicians, of the businessmen, of the journalists, of the police, of the judiciary and of the 'authorities' – that is, anyone who, according to their opponents, thought they knew better than you did. They were the members of the 'establishment'.

The GLF was established or, rather, came together in Highbury Fields, in November 1970, largely as a reaction against a dubious arrest in a public urinal. It was borne out of rage, and defiance, against harassment. In the month before some students had agreed to attend weekly meetings at the London School of Economics, partly in response to the 'Stonewall' riots of New York in the summer of 1969. In the manifesto of the GLF the demand for equality was accompanied by a rejection of discrimination. In the summer of 1972 the first Gay Pride march was held. Its colourful supporters walked from Trafalgar Square to Hyde Park; in various incarnations it has continued ever since. *Gay News* was first published in that summer, testifying to the broader sense of community and self-assertion in those who were even then learning to be called and to call themselves 'gay'. Coincidentally or not – it is said that in London there is no such thing as coincidence – *Spare Rib*, the first radical feminist magazine of its type, was established at the same time. More than one bookshop catering for gay readers opened in London.

Like many altruistic endeavours the Gay Liberation Front came to pieces in the end, shipwrecked by internal dissension and recrimination. It was divided largely between the different aspirations of men and women, between those who supported active and radical protests and those who did not, between the socialists or the New Left and various anti-authoritarian or counter-cultural movements. Some preferred flower power while others campaigned for street power. The GLF could not contain its contradictions. But its legacy remained in the number of subgroups such as the Gay Black Group and the Gay Teenage Group, as well as in the less tangible but equally significant new mood of resolution and independence among queer men.

Not all queer men were enthusiastic about the sudden exit from the closet; some thought it in bad taste, while others were simply alienated by the pack mentality which solidarity sometimes espoused. It was all too grim and self-righteous for many of the less committed. For others, however, the burgeoning of GLF meetings, gatherings and parades offered the opportunity for picking up sexual partners outside the claustrophobic atmosphere of clubs and pubs. Yet many others still, perhaps the majority, lacked the self-confidence openly to proclaim themselves in the face of a hostile or indifferent public. They did not wish to rock the boat.

Yet ironically it was the movement towards queer liberation that helped to prompt the extraordinary growth in nightclubs in London; these tended to be multi-levelled discotheques in which dazzling light and sound helped to encourage an atmosphere of fevered sexuality. In 1976 Bang! was opened on Monday nights at the Astoria off Tottenham Court Road, and was soon succeeded by others in the vicinity and elsewhere. The thumping beat of disco music and the gyrations of scantily clad customers helped to define a movement of hedonism and consumerism that seemed set to define queer London of the 1980s.

And then the music stopped.

By 1982 there were rumours of a new illness. The year before, five young men had succumbed to a rare form of pneumonia in Los Angeles; in the summer of the following year Terrence Higgins died in St Thomas's Hospital, London, of what seemed to be a related condition. The bad news was at first greeted with disbelief and even denial. It was an American disease. It would pass. A cure would soon be found. All of these bland prognostications faltered as the condition spread wider still and wider. It soon became known as 'gay men's cancer' and then, as its virulence increased, 'the gay plague'. As information about its nature spread it was known more neutrally as Aids or 'acquired immune deficiency syndrome'. Suddenly everyone knew what the 'immune system' was and what its 'deficiency' meant.

This new condition seemed to stalk gay men, inducing horror, helplessness and confusion. The varieties of symptoms were endlessly discussed in an atmosphere where panic was mingled with ignorance. It became known that some forms of Aids led to blindness, others to skin cancer and still others to pneumonia. The newspapers took delight in publishing photographs of gaunt, emaciated men.

The earliest sufferers were often stigmatised. They became outcasts, abused or ignored by the general population and treated only with extreme nervousness and caution by the medical profession. Many dentists were suddenly unavailable and most medical procedures were accompanied by precautions that resembled the after-effects of a nuclear explosion. Aids appeared to be a death sentence and, perhaps because many of its victims were very young, there were few means of coping with dying. Aids induced fear, depression and almost constant panic. There was, for many, nothing ahead except darkness.

When it began to hit friends and acquaintances, the reality became almost too great to bear. The symptoms were feverishness, trembling, shuddering and sweating, failing sight, disabling diarrhoea, or general nervous lassitude. The only palliatives were painkillers, self-administered injections, endless pills of unknown provenance, tubes, injections; the regular visits to the hospitals were of course demeaning enough, but not so bad as the periods in the wards where you might lie beside a bed in which a young man was curled up in preparation for death. Fellow sufferers served only to intensify the misery. It was as if they were neither living nor dead. The feeling of helplessness was increased by the suspicion that the prescribed medicines themselves were responsible for some of the more morbid symptoms. Did the doctors know what they were doing?

The general and public reaction was largely one of indifference or even hostility. It was believed that queer men 'had brought it on themselves', that it 'was all their own fault' and that they 'deserved it'. Attacks on queer men did not diminish in intensity. The level of public hostility was emphasised in 1988 by the Conservative government's introduction of Clause 28 into the Local Government Act which decreed that 'a local authority shall not (a) intentionally promote homosexuality or publish material with the intention of promoting homosexuality; (b) promote the teaching in any maintained school of the acceptability of homosexuality as a pretended family relationship'. One columnist in *The Times* declared that 'this country seems to be in a galloping frenzy of hate, where homosexuals are concerned, that will soon, if it is not checked, lead to something like a pogrom'.

The queer reaction to the bigotry was one of understandable fury, but it was now alleviated by one small consolation. The horrors of the Aids epidemic, and the need for voluntary cooperation in trying to deal with the effects of the condition, had lent a sense of communal identity to many of those who might otherwise have gone separate ways. Some were enraged by what they considered to be the insufficient official response to the crisis, and saw Clause 28 as another attack upon the rights of what by then had become known as the 'gay community' – even though many queer males and females would have been horrified to be considered a 'community' at all. Now there emerged a sense of belonging, and of real if unspoken common humanity.

And then the band began to play again . . .

The incidence of mortality among the sufferers of Aids had abated, and new forms of treatment had become available to allay the worst symptoms of the condition. This amounted on occasion to complacency, as if the epidemic had never happened. The clubs and bars were more crowded than ever, and some previous activists lamented the fact that the once libertarian and radical aspects of queer liberation had been subsumed by a generally capitalist and consumerist culture. Many men and women felt excluded by queer liberation, alienated by the emphasis on youth, fashion and good looks. Perhaps it has always been thus. The effects of Clause 28 were, as it turned out, minimal; its most important consequence lay in the self-definition of those who protested against it. As the London newspaper *Capital Gay* put it, 'the visibility of our community has rarely, if ever, been greater'. In February 1994 the age of sexual consent for queer men was lowered to eighteen and then, six years later, to sixteen. In that year, 2000, the ban on queers serving in the military was finally lifted. What had once been barred or banned was now accepted and welcomed.

In the spirit of tolerance, same-sex civil partnerships and marriages are now condoned and even encouraged. Recent surveys have indicated that queer couples now seek the permanent union of marriage for the same reasons as their parents or grandparents; they are eager for love and commitment. They want ordinary lives based on loyalty and intimacy. This is a long way from the activism of Stonewall. There is now no question of estrangement from the larger society or of the reinvention of cultural and sexual identity.

So, gradually but inexorably, gay London has become part of the normal world and a corner of the Western playground of Europe. Bars have emerged on many street corners of central London with no ambiguity at all about the inclinations of their clients; they have large plate-glass windows rather than the closed doors and barred windows of the twentieth century. Their customers spill onto the streets. Some areas of London, most notably Old Compton Street in Soho, have become gay zones. Gay newspapers, gay magazines and gay switchboards for multifarious purposes have sprung up, together with gay accountants, gay builders and gay undertakers. It would be no cause for wonder to find a gay fish-and-chip shop or a gay abattoir.

In the last few decades academic interest has become focused on what has become known as 'queer theory'. Much of it was established upon postmodern versions of 'construction' and 'performance', 'narratives' and 'scripts'. It is a new way of devising questions for old problems.

The abiding question is also the most ancient. Are queers born or are they made? The 'essentialists' suppose that homosexuality is a fixed and universal component of the human condition; 'constructivists' believe that it is a cultural invention that responds to various social and political initiatives. A definitive answer has yet to be found but, in the meantime, very few outside the academic community seem preoccupied with the dilemma. The matter has in fact been complicated by the emergence of other types of sexuality including transgender and transsexualism. Those who cultivate and foster the transgender life are involved in what might be called existential change; those who decide upon practical and surgical intervention merit the name of transsexuals. It is an ambiguous distinction – but in this realm ambiguity rules.

One of the most significant developments in recent years has been the increasing incidence of those who reject their presumed gender. Many do not believe that they belong to the gender to which they were assigned at birth; some decide actively to change it by means of surgery; others defy it by dress and behaviour. Others do not subscribe to the concept of sexual difference in the first place, arguing that time, circumstance and opportunity prevail rather than stereotypes of gender. It is possible, even likely, that people without a fixed gender or stable sexual identity have always existed but have been ignored or unnoticed for many London generations. In the early years of the twenty-first century, at last they have been granted recognition and identity. They have come of age. The apparent change in popular stereotypes (though not necessarily obvious in popular culture) is now exemplified by openly gay politicians, gay singers, gay comics (who can be very gay indeed), gay writers, gay sports stars, recent transgender celebrities, and transgender people in the sciences.

2013 was one of the most significant years. Civil marriage between partners of the same sex was amplified by the rite of marriage itself. The law was passed without a change to the legal definition of marriage. The prime minister, David Cameron, sought to soothe the apparent contradiction of a Conservative government supporting such a move. He declared that he believed in gay marriage not 'in spite of being a Conservative, but because I am a Conservative'. The former Archbishop of Canterbury, Dr Carey, warned that the meaning of marriage would change, and that no single body, neither the state nor the Church, 'owned' marriage.

Maureen Le Marinel, a gay woman, became president of Unison, one of Britain's largest unions. Paris Lee, a trans woman noted for her lively political journalism, became the first transgender person to appear on *Question Time*. In the same year Nikki Sinclaire became the United Kingdom's first openly transgender parliamentarian in Europe and Lucy Vallender the first transgender woman to convert to Islam. As a result of these actions the visibility of trans people has strengthened noticeably over the last few years.

In 2014 the same-sex marriage law came into effect. The marriage of Nicola Pettit and Tania Ward represented Britain's first Jewish gay women's union. *Boy Meets Girl*, a situation comedy about transgender people, was commissioned by BBC2, a reminder that social change has been actively promoted by television and other media. Amid all this the Queen found time to issue her personal congratulations to the London Lesbian and Gay Switchboard on its fortieth anniversary. It is a measure of quite how far the gay community has entered the respectable fold not merely that its oldest organ should receive royal endorsement, but that that endorsement should be offered by a monarch who takes her duties to the established Church very seriously indeed.

In 2015, Mikhail Ivan Gallatinov married Marc Goodwin, the first such marriage to be held in a prison; Laverne Cox received the signal favour of a statue in Madame Tussauds. In the field of sport Sam Stanley became the first Rugby Union player to come out as gay. The television soap opera *EastEnders* introduced Riley Carter Millington, one of the first openly transgender actors in British 'soap' history. In a bold and for many disquieting move, the BBC aired the performance of a phalloplasty.

Trans people, whether or not they have undergone any sort of transition, represent a tiny portion of the population. Here, however, questions of gender 'fluidity' arise. The current acronym for queer society as a whole is no longer LGBT but LGBTQIA – an expansion from 'lesbian gay bisexual transgender' to include 'queer intersex asexual'. Queer in this context means those who are unsure of their sexual identity, while intersex means those having the primary or secondary sexual characteristics of both genders. This list will no doubt grow.

But the question is bedevilled by the fact that for a long time sexuality itself has been seen as a matter of identity. Gore Vidal maintained that there are no heterosexual or homosexual people, only heterosexual or homosexual acts. This was unexceptionable at the time; now it would be considered almost reactionary. The rise of social media is of some significance. 'Identity politics', once a somewhat arcane movement local to university campuses, now has social media as its forum, especially with regard to questions of sexuality or gender identity. Many people eminent in the conventional media have found themselves attacked on the 'blogosphere' or on Twitter for failing to recognise new orthodoxies of expression. Sometimes the matter becomes more public and more serious.

The last decade has at one level been a quiet period for the queer community. Its contours have been soft, its colours tending to the sepia. The great gay scandals of the last century are largely absent, perhaps partly because to be gay is no longer a scandal. What was once termed the gay 'scene' is a more muted affair than that which existed twenty years ago. The expression itself, 'scene', with its connotations of performance and abandon, is now rarely used.

The picture, at first or even second glance, is not a vibrant one. Bars and clubs, which might once have been termed louche, are fast closing or becoming 'safer'. The brocade of Old Compton Street seems to be fraying yearly. The Candy Bar, once the hub of London's lesbian scene, closed in 2014. Its quondam owners swiftly opened a replacement but this, KU Girls, is only an adjunct to its male counterpart on the ground floor. The drag venue once considered the ruby in Soho's crown, Madame Jojo's, was shut down in 2014 after a violent altercation outside its doors. The Admiral Duncan in Old Compton Street, bombed in a homophobic attack of 1999, still flies the LGBT flag, but its old panache is scarcely discernible.

The City of Quebec, arguably London's oldest gay bar, still has its affectionate devotees. It is instructive, if not saddening, to note that one younger visitor to its website commented: 'I didn't know it was gay.' Of many former queer venues, not a rack is left behind. The Play Pen in Notting Hill, the favoured haunt of impecunious aristocrats in the illegal as well as illicit days, has long vanished. Nevertheless the Royal Vauxhall Tavern is still thriving. In fact Vauxhall has in many ways taken the place of Soho as the 'gay village' of London – in consort with the Vauxhall Gardens of the eighteenth century.

The substantial lesson of the past decade is that queerness, with all its panache and ferocity, is in elegant retreat. A possible exception is Hampstead Heath, a *locus amoenus* for generations of queer Londoners who found the combination of bushes, trees and long grass irresistible. It flourishes still. While it would be an exaggeration to conclude that the queer world is in terminal decline, it is certainly in a process of reinvention. 'Cruise bars' are increasingly open only to members, saunas are increasingly clean (Continental visitors to queer England have austere standards), and bars no longer have back rooms which remain open after public rooms have closed. More importantly, a dichotomy has emerged between those venues that bellow and those that whisper, those that are openly gay and those that are merely 'gay-friendly'.

This is paradigmatic of a fundamental and long-standing dilemma: the queer community has never quite made up its mind whether it desires or fears integration. This ambivalence has been thrown into relief by the passage of several parliamentary acts. With the right to marry and adopt, gay people seem less involved with the rush and roll of cruising and carousing than they were thirty years ago and are more concerned with settling down within a domestic environment. A clear link is emerging; with the opportunities for marriage beckoning, the need for an aggressive counter-culture has dwindled. Legal acceptance has bred a certain placidity. This can be seen in the way that some cities, Liverpool, Birmingham and Manchester among them, have gay 'villages' which are, on the whole, pedestrianised to create a human space. It is not altogether surprising that England's 'Lesbian capital' should be the quiet trans-Pennine village of Hebden Bridge, where female couples raise their children side by side with an easy-going local community.

But violence and prejudice still abound. In some cities the gay and trans communities have suffered several attacks over the past few years. 'Coming out' is still a rite of passage, frequently characterised by trauma. Where sixty years ago homosexuality itself was a crime, homophobia has now taken its place, and the very expression 'coming out' testifies to lingering societal prejudice.

The process by which poor or neglected areas are galvanised and renovated by the wealthy – a process rather lazily termed 'gentrification' – is one to which gay people have usually been pivotal. It seems, however, that this very gift for improving an area has turned on these pioneers. Soho, for example, is indeed too expensive now to afford much genuine bohemianism. The solution, once again, is simply to look further afield – into Whitechapel, Spitalfields and beyond.

As the history of religion shows, people are never more contentious than when the source of their quarrel is something unfalsifiable. Here is where the notion of a queer 'spectrum' has proved unhelpful: when the meaning, if any, of a term is uncertain, it will be fought over. The increasing preference for a notion of gender 'fluidity' itself accounts not only for the almost bewildering array of terms now approved within debates about gender identity, but also for the remarkably ad hominem or ad feminam sparring that takes place in social media. The initially puzzling exhortation to 'Check your privilege!' is, at its best, merely an appeal for a recognition that our opinions can be rooted in personal circumstances that not everyone is heir to. Thus a white middle-class woman is not best placed to lecture a working-class black woman, or vice versa. When the question turns to gender identity, however, something farcical can ensue. A 'cis woman' (one born a woman in gender as well as in sexual characteristics) will tell a trans woman to check her privilege for having been able to avoid the difficulties of growing up a woman; a trans woman will retort that the cis woman should check her own privilege for not having undergone all the agonies entailed by growing up in the wrong biological sex, or for never having confronted transphobia. So it goes on.

William Blake put it best in 1809 when he noted that 'Accident ever varies, Substance can never suffer change nor decay'. He stated this in the context of Chaucer's London pilgrims, some of them not so different from the sexual pilgrims followed in this book. And, as Blake added, 'the characters themselves remain for ever unaltered . . . Names alter, things never alter.' In truth there are many sexes in London. There have always been many sexes in the city. This book is a celebration, as well as a history, of the continual and various human world maintained in its diversity despite persecution, condemnation and affliction. It represents the ultimate triumph of London.

Acknowledgements

I am grateful to my research assistants, Thomas Wright and Murrough O'Brien, for their assistance on this volume. I am particularly grateful to Murrough O'Brien for furnishing details of the contemporary urban scene.

Bibliography

Ackroyd, P., *Dressing up, Transvestism and Drag: The History of an Obsession* (London, 1979)

Aldrich, R. (ed.), *Gay Life and Culture: A World History* (London, 2006)

Altman, D. (ed.), *Homosexuality, which homosexuality?* (Amsterdam, 1989)

Andreadis, A. H., *Sappho in Early Modern England: Female Same-Sex Literary Erotics, 1550–1714* (Chicago, 2001)

Andrei, C., *Transgender Underground: London & the Third Sex* (London, 2002)

Anon, *Hell upon Earth: Or the Town in an Uproar. Occasion'd by the Late Horrible Scenes of Forgery, Perjury, Street-robbery, Murder, Sodomy, and other Shocking Impieties . . .* (London, 1729)

Anon, *Select Trials, for Murders, Robberies, Rapes, Sodomy, Coining, Frauds, and other offences at the Sessions-House in the Old-Bailey . . .* (London, 1742)

Arnold, C., *City of Sin: London and its Vices* (London, 2010)

Aronson, T., *Prince Eddy and the Homosexual Underworld* (London, 1994)

Bailey, D. S., *Homosexuality and the Western Christian Tradition* (London, 1955)

Bartlett, N., *Who was that Man? A Present for Mr. Oscar Wilde* (London, 1988)

Beckford, W., *Life at Fonthill, 1807–1822* (Stroud, 2006)

Bell, D., & Valentine, G., *Mapping Desire: Geographies of Sexualities* (London, 1995)

Bellamy, J. G., *Crime and Public Order in England in the Later Middle Ages* (London, 1973)

Bergeron, D. M., *King James and Letters of Homoerotic Desire* (Iowa, 1999)

Betteridge, T. (ed.), *Sodomy in Early Modern Europe* (Manchester, 2002)

Bly, M., *Queer Virgins and Virgin Queans on the Early Modern Stage* (Oxford, 2000)

Borris, K., *Same-Sex Desire in the English Renaissance: A Sourcebook of Texts, 1470–1650* (New York, 2003)

Boswell, J., *Christianity, Social Tolerance, and Homosexuality: Gay People in Western Europe from the Beginning of the Christian Era to the Fourteenth Century* (Chicago, 1980)

Boswell, J., *The Marriage of Likeness: Same-Sex Unions in Pre-Modern Europe* (London, 1995)

Boucé, P-G. (ed.), *Sexuality in eighteenth-century Britain* (Manchester, 1982)

Brady, S., *Masculinity and Male Homosexuality in Britain, 1861–1913* (New York, 2005)

Bray, A., *Homosexuality in Renaissance England* (London, 1982)

Bray, A., *The Friend* (Chicago, 2003)

Bredbeck, G. W., *Sodomy and Interpretation: Marlowe to Milton* (Ithaca, 1991)

Bromley, J. M., & Stockton, W. (eds), *Sex Before Sex: Figuring the Act in Early Modern England* (Minneapolis, 2013)

Brown, J., *Trapped: Living with Gender Dysphoria* (Milton Keynes, 2008)

Bullough, V. L., *Sexual Variance in Society and History* (New York, 1976)

Bullough, V. L., & Brundage, J. A. (eds), *Handbook of Medieval Sexuality* (New York, 1996)

Burford, E. J., *The Orrible Synne: A Look at London Lechery from Roman to Cromwellian times* (London, 1973)

Burke, T., *The London Spy: A Book of Town Travels* (London, 1922)

Chaplais, P., *Piers Gaveston: Edward II's Adoptive Brother* (Oxford, 1994)

Clark, D., *Between Medieval Men: Male Friendship and Desire in Early Medieval English Literature* (Oxford, 2013)

Cocks, H., *Nameless Offences: Homosexual Desire in the 19th Century* (London, 2003)

Cocks, H., & Houlbrook, M. (eds), *Palgrave Advances in the Modern History of Sexuality* (Basingstoke, 2006)

Cohen, E., *Talk on the Wilde Side: Towards a Genealogy of a Discourse on Male Sexualities* (New York, 1993)

Cohen, J. J., & Wheeler, B. (eds), *Becoming Male in the Middle Ages* (New York, 1997)

Cook, M., *London and the Culture of Homosexuality, 1885–1914* (Cambridge, 2003)

Cook, M., *Queer Domesticities: Homosexuality and Home Life in Twentieth-Century London* (Basingstoke, 2014)

Cook, M., Cocks, H., Mills, R., & Trumbach, R. (eds), *A Gay History of Britain: Love and Sex between Men since the Middle Ages* (Oxford, 2007)

Crawford, K., *European Sexualities, 1400–1800* (Cambridge, 2007)

Crisp, Q., *The Naked Civil Servant* (London, 1977)

Crompton, L., *Byron and Greek love: Homophobia in 19th-century England* (London, 1985)

Crompton, L., *Homosexuality and Civilization* (Cambridge, MA, 2003)

Cruickshank, D., *The Secret History of Georgian London: How the Wages of Sin Shaped the Capital* (London, 2009)

Davenport-Hines, R. P. T., *Sex, Death and Punishment: Attitudes to Sex and Sexuality in Britain Since the Renaissance* (London, 1990)

David, H., *On Queer Street: A Social History of British Homosexuality, 1895–1995* (London, 1997)

Dekker, R., & Pol, L. van de, *The Tradition of Female Transvestism in Early Modern Europe* (Basingstoke, 1989)

Dellamora, R., *Victorian Sexual Dissidence* (Chicago, 1999)

Dinshaw, C., *Getting Medieval: Sexualities and Communities, Pre- and Postmodern* (Durham, NC, 1999)

DiPiero, T., & Gill, P. (eds), *Illicit Sex: Identity Politics in Early Modern Culture* (Athens, GA, 1996)

Doan, L. L., *Fashioning Sapphism: The Origins of a Modern English Lesbian Culture* (New York, 2001)
Donoghue, E. (ed.), *Passions Between Women* (London, 2014)
Duberman, M. B., Vicinus, M., & Chauncey, G., *Hidden from History: Reclaiming the Gay and Lesbian Past* (London, 1991)
Ekins, R., & King, D., *The Transgender Phenomenon* (London, 2006)
Ellis, H., *Studies in the Psychology of Sex (Vol. II): Sexual Inversion* (Philadelphia, 1921)
Epstein, J., & Straub, K. (eds), *Body Guards: The Cultural Politics of Gender Ambiguity* (New York, 1991)
Faderman, L., *Surpassing the Love of Men: Romantic Friendship and Love between Women from the Renaissance to the Present* (London, 1985)
Farnham, M., & Marshall, P., *Walking after Midnight: Gay Men's Life Stories* (London, 1989)
Fielding, H., *The Female Husband: Or, the Surprising History of Mrs. Mary, Alias Mr. George Hamilton, who was Convicted of having Married a Young Woman of Wells and Lived with her as her Husband. Taken from her own Mouth since her Confinement* (London, 1746)
Fletcher, A., *Gender, Sex and Subordination in England, 1500–1800* (New Haven, 1995)
Forster, E. M., *Maurice* (London, 1971)
Foucault, M., *The History of Sexuality*, 3 volumes (Harmondsworth, 1990)
Fradenburg, L. O. A., & Freccero, C., (eds), *Premodern Sexualities* (New York, 1996)
Frantzen, A. J., *Before the Closet: Same-Sex Love from Beowulf to Angels in America* (Chicago, 1998)
Garton, S., *Histories of Sexuality* (London, 2004)
Gerard, K., & Hekma, G., *The Pursuit of Sodomy: Male Homosexuality in Renaissance and Enlightenment Europe* (New York, 1989)
Goldberg, J., *Sodometries: Renaissance Texts, Modern Sexualities* (Stanford, 1992)
Goldberg, J. (ed.), *Queering the Renaissance* (Durham, NC, 1994)
Goldberg, J. (ed.), *Reclaiming Sodom* (New York, 1994)

Goldsmith, N. M., *The Worst of Crimes: Homosexuality and the Law in Eighteenth-century London* (Aldershot, 1998)

Goodich, M., *The Unmentionable Vice: Homosexuality in the Later Medieval Period* (Santa Barbara, 1979)

Greenberg, D. F., *The Construction of Homosexuality* (Chicago, 1988)

Hadley, D. M., *Masculinity in Medieval Europe* (London, 1999)

Haggerty, G. E., *Men in Love: Masculinity and Sexuality in the Eighteenth Century* (New York, 1999)

Haggerty, G. E., *Queer Gothic* (Urbana, 2006)

Hall, R., *The Well of Loneliness* (London, 1973)

Hallam, P., *The Book of Sodom* (London, 1993)

Halperin, D. M., *One Hundred Years of Homosexuality: And Other Essays on Greek Love* (New York, 1990)

Halsband, R., *Lord Hervey; Eighteenth-Century Courtier* (Oxford, 1973)

Hammond, P., *Figuring Sex between Men from Shakespeare to Rochester* (Oxford, 2002)

Harris, M., *The Dilly Boys: Male Prostitution in Piccadilly* (London, 1973)

Harrison, M., *The London That Was Rome* (London, 1971)

Harvey, A. D., *Sex in Georgian England: Attitudes and Prejudices from the 1720s to the 1820s* (London, 1994)

Heaphy, B., Smart, C., & Einarsdottir, A., *Same Sex Marriages: New Generations, New Relationships* (Basingstoke, 2013)

Herdt, G. H., *Third Sex, Third Gender: Beyond Sexual Dimorphism in Culture and History* (New York, 1994)

Hergemöller, B-U., & Phillips, J., *Sodom and Gomorrah: On the Everyday Reality and Persecution of Homosexuals in the Middle Ages* (London, 2001)

Herrup, C. B., *A House in Gross Disorder: Sex, Law, and the 2nd Earl of Castlehaven* (New York, 1999)

Higgins, P., *Heterosexual Dictatorship: Male Homosexuality in Postwar Britain* (London, 1996)

Higgs, D. (ed.), *Queer Sites: Gay Urban Histories since 1600* (London, 1999)

Hitchcock, T., *English Sexualities, 1700–1800* (Basingstoke, 1997)

Hitchcock, T., & Cohen, M. (ed.), *English Masculinities, 1660–1800* (London, 1999)

Holloway, R., *The Phoenix of Sodom* (Portsmouth, 2011)

Houlbrook, M., *Queer London: Perils and Pleasures in the Sexual Metropolis, 1918–1957* (Chicago, 2005)

Hyde, H. M., *The Other Love: An Historical and Contemporary Survey of Homosexuality in Britain* (London, 1970)

Hyde, H. M., *The Cleveland Street Scandal* (London, 1976)

Janes, D., *Picturing the Closet: Male Secrecy and Homosexual Visibility in Britain* (Oxford, 2015)

Jennings, R., *A Lesbian History of Britain: Love and Sex between Women since 1500* (Oxford, 2007)

Jordan, M. D., *The Invention of Sodomy in Christian Theology* (Chicago, 1997)

Kaplan, M. B., *Sodom on the Thames: Sex, Love, and Scandal in Wilde Times* (Ithaca, 2005)

Keiser, E. B., *Courtly Desire and Medieval Homophobia: The Legitimation of Sexual Pleasure in Cleanness and its Contexts* (New Haven, 1997)

Kellow, C., *The Victorian Underworld* (Harmondsworth, 1972)

Ketton-Cremer, R. W., *Thomas Gray: A Biography* (Cambridge, 1955)

King, T. A., *The Gendering of Men, 1600–1750, Volume 1: The English Phallus* (Madison, 2004)

Koven, S., *Slumming: Sexual and Social Politics in Victorian London* (Princeton, 2004)

Laslett, P., *The World we have Lost* (London, 1965)

Lewis, B. (ed.), *British Queer History: New Approaches and Perspectives* (Manchester, 2013)

Linnane, F., *London: The Wicked City: A Thousand Years of Vice in the Capital* (London, 2003)

Maccubbin, R. P. (ed.), *'Tis Nature's Fault: Unauthorized Sexuality during the Enlightenment* (Cambridge, 1987)

McCormick, I. (ed.), *Secret Sexualities: A Sourcebook of 17th and 18th Century Writing* (London, 1997)

McKenna, N., *The Secret Life of Oscar Wilde* (London, 2003)

McKenna, N., *Fanny and Stella: The Young Men who Shocked Victorian England* (London, 2013)

Mayne, X., *Intersexes: a History of Similisexualism As a Problem in Social Life* (Geneva, *c.*1909)

Miller, N., *Out of the Past: Gay and Lesbian History from 1869 to the Present* (London, 1995)

Mounsey, C., *Presenting Gender: Changing Sex in Early-Modern Culture* (Lewisburg, PA, 2001)

Mounsey, C., & Gonda, C. (eds), *Queer People: Negotiations and Expressions of Homosexuality, 1700–1800* (Lewisburg, PA, 2007)

Murray, J., *Conflicted Identities and Multiple Masculinities: Men in the Medieval West* (New York, 1999)

Murray, J., & Eisenbichler, K. (eds), *Desire and Discipline: Sex and Sexuality in the Premodern West* (Toronto, 1996)

Naphy, W. G., *Born to be Gay: A History of Homosexuality* (Stroud, 2004)

Norton, R., *Mother Clap's Molly House: The Gay Subculture in England 1700–1830* (London, 1992)

Norton, R., *The Myth of the Modern Homosexual: Queer History and the Search for Cultural Unity* (London, 1997)

Norton, R., *Gay History and Literature* (London, 2016)

Norton, R. (ed.), *Homosexuality in Eighteenth-Century England: A Sourcebook* (London, 2016)

O'Donnell, K., & O'Rourke, M. (eds), *Love, Sex, Intimacy, and Friendship between Men, 1550–1800* (Basingstoke, 2003)

Oram, A., & Turnbull, A. (eds), *The Lesbian History Sourcebook: Love and Sex between Women in Britain from 1780 to 1970* (London, 2001)

Orgel, S., *Impersonations: The Performance of Gender in Shakespeare's England* (Cambridge, 1996)

Orton, J., *The Orton Diaries: Including the Correspondence of Edna Welthorpe and Others* (Lahr, J., ed.) (London, 1986)

Pasternack, C. B., & Weston, L. M. (eds), *Sex and Sexuality in Anglo-Saxon England: Essays in Memory of Daniel Gillmore Calder* (Tempe, AZ, 2004)

Payer, P. J., *Sex and the Penitentials: The Development of a Sexual Code, 550–1150* (Toronto, 1984)

Peakman, J., *Lascivious Bodies: A Sexual History of the Eighteenth Century* (London, 2004)

Phillips, K. M., & Reay, B., *Sexualities in History: A Reader* (New York, 2002)

Phillips, K. M., & Reay, B., *Sex Before Sexuality: A Premodern History* (Cambridge, 2011)

Plummer, K. (ed.), *The Making of the Modern Homosexual* (London, 1981)

Porter, K., & Weeks, J. (eds), *Between the Acts: Lives of Homosexual Men 1885–1967* (London, 1991)

Porter, R., & Rousseau, G. S. (eds), *Sexual Underworlds of the Enlightenment* (Manchester, 1987)

Quinn, P. A., *Better than the Sons of Kings: Boys and Monks in the Early Middle Ages* (New York, 1989)

Raitt, S. (ed.), *Volcanoes and Pearl Divers: Essays in Lesbian Feminist Studies* (London, 1995)

Reade, B. (ed.), *Sexual Heretics: Male Homosexuality in English Literature from 1850 to 1900: An Anthology* (London, 1970)

Render, R. (ed.), *A Narrative of the Life of Mrs. Charlotte Clarke* (London, 1999)

Robb, G., & Erber, N., (eds), *Disorder in the Court: Trials and Sexual Conflict at the Turn of the Century* (Basingstoke, 1999)

Robinson, P., *The Changing World of Gay Men* (Basingstoke, 2008)

Rocke, M., *Forbidden Friendships: Homosexuality and Male Culture in Renaissance Florence* (New York, 1996)

Rossiaud, J., & Cochrane, L. G., *Medieval Prostitution* (Oxford, 1988)

Rowland, J. T., *'Swords in myrtle dress'd': Towards a Rhetoric of Sodom: Gay Readings of Homosexual Politics and Poetics in the Eighteenth Century* (Madison, 1998)

Sedgwick, E. K., *Between Men: English Literature and Male Homosocial Desire* (New York, 1985)

Simpson, C., Chester, L., & Leitch, D., *The Cleveland Street Affair* (London, 1977)

Sinfield, A., *The Wilde Century: Effeminacy, Oscar Wilde and the Queer Moment* (London, 1994)

Smith, B. R., *Homosexual Desire in Shakespeare's England: A Cultural Poetics* (Chicago, 1991)

Spencer, C., *Homosexuality: A History* (London, 1995)

Stearns, P. N., *Sexuality in World History* (London, 2009)

Steele, E., *The Memoirs of Mrs Sophia Baddeley, Late of Drury Lane Theatre* (London, 1787)

Steele, V., *A Queer History of Fashion: From the Closet to the Catwalk* (New Haven, 2013)

Stewart, A., *Close Readers: Humanism and Sodomy in Early Modern England* (Princeton, 1997)

Summers, C. J. (ed.), *Homosexuality in Renaissance and Enlightenment England: Literary Representation in Historical Context* (New York, 1992)

Summerskill, C., *Gateway to Heaven: Fifty Years of Lesbian and Gay Oral History* (London, 2013)

Todd, J., *The Secret Life of Aphra Behn* (London, 1996)

Toulalan, S., *Imagining Sex: Pornography and Bodies in Seventeenth-Century England* (Oxford, 2007)

Trumbach, R., *Sex and the Gender Revolution* (Chicago, 1998)

Vicinus, M., *Intimate Friends: Women Who Loved Women: 1778–1928* (Chicago, 2004)

Walton, T. (ed.), *Out of the Shadows: A History of the Pioneering London Gay Groups and Organisations, 1967–2000* (London, 2010)

Weeks, J., *Coming Out: Homosexual Politics in Britain, from the Nineteenth Century to the Present* (London, 1990)

Weeks, J., *The World We Have Won: The Remaking of Erotic and Intimate Life* (London, 2007)

Whitaker, K., *Mad Madge* (London, 2003)

White, C. (ed.), *Nineteenth-Century Writings on Homosexuality: A Sourcebook* (London, 1999)

Whittle, S. (ed.), *The Margins of the City: Gay Men's Urban Lives* (Aldershot, 1994)

Wilson, E., *The Sphinx in the City: Urban Life, the Control of Disorder, and Women* (London, 1991)

Wilson, W., *Love-letters between a Certain Late Nobleman and the Famous Mr. Wilson* (London, 1723)

Wunderli, R. M., *London Church Courts and Society on the Eve of the Reformation* (Cambridge, MA, 1981)

Young, M. B., *James VI and I and the History of Homosexuality* (Basingstoke, 2000)

Zeikowitz, R. E., *Homoeroticism and Chivalry: Discourses in Male Same-Sex Desire in the Fourteenth Century* (New York, 2003)

Zimmerman, S. (ed.), *Erotic Politics: Desire on the Renaissance Stage* (New York, 1992)

Index